THE PENGUIN BOOK OF JOKES

collected by Phillip Adams and Patrice Newell

Phillip Adams is a writer, broadcaster and filmmaker. He helped with the small child and the olive trees.

Patrice Newell is a former model, television researcher, presenter of public affairs programmes and now manages a small child and a large bio-dynamic farm in the Hunter Valley. This year she planted 2000 olive trees.

Phillip Adams and Patrice Newell are the authors of the joke collections *The Penguin Book of Australian Jokes*, *The Penguin Book of More Australian Jokes*, and *The Penguin Book of Jokes from Cyberspace*.

THE PENGUIN BOOK OF SCHOOLYARD JOKES

collected by Phillip Adams
and Patrice Newell

Penguin Books

Penguin Books Australia Ltd
487 Maroondah Highway, P.O. Box 257
Ringwood, Victoria 3134, Australia
Penguin Books Ltd
Harmondsworth, Middlesex, England
Viking Penguin, A Division of Penguin Books USA Inc.
375 Hudson Street, New York, New York 10014, USA
Penguin Books Canada Limited
10 Alcorn Avenue, Toronto, Ontario, Canada M4V 3B2
Penguin Books (N.Z.) Ltd
Cnr Rosedale and Airborne Roads, Albany, Auckland, New Zealand

First published by Penguin Books Australia Ltd 1997

10 9 8 7 6 5 4 3 2 1

This selection, introduction and other original material © Phillip Adams and Patrice Newell, 1997

All rights reserved. Without limiting the rights under copyright reserved above, no part of this publication may be reproduced, stored in or introduced into a retrieval system, or transmitted, in any form or by any means (electronic, mechanical, photocopying, recording or otherwise), without the prior written permission of both the copyright owner and the above publisher of this book.

Cover illustration by Ned Culic

Typeset by Midland Typesetters, Maryborough, Victoria
Designed by Glenn Thomas, Penguin Design Studio
Printed and bound in Australia by Australian Print Group

National Library of Australia
Cataloguing-in-Publication data:
The Penguin book of schoolyard jokes.

Includes index.
ISBN 014 027 1945.

1. Australian wit and humour. I. Adams, Phillip, 1939– .
II. Newell, Patrice, 1956– . III. Title: Book of schoolyard jokes.

A 828.02

ACKNOWLEDGEMENTS

Hundreds of children across Australia contributed to this collection. Special thanks go to our technical advisers, Vidas Kubilius, Vavia Kubilius and Rory Adams.

And a huge thank you to all the teachers and school kids who sent us jokes and gave us lots of laughs, especially Scone Public School; St Mary's, Scone; St James, Muswellbrook; Mullumbimby Adventist Primary School and Colonel Light Gardens Primary School.

Contents

A Few Words to the Grown-ups 1
Animal Antics 11
Family Life 85
Fatty & Skinny 107
Food, Glorious Food 111
Heffalumps 153
Knock Knock 165
Medical Matters 191
Multiculturalism 205
Naughtiness 215
Oddities & Insults 223
People 241
Riddles 251
Scary Stories 293
School Days 331
Sporting Events 345
What Do You Call . . . ? 353
Word Play 359
Index 371

A FEW WORDS TO THE GROWN-UPS

When introducing our first collection of jokes for Penguin we speculated on the origins and evolutionary purpose of humour. While the experts passionately disagreed, as experts tend to do, there seemed to be a scholarly consensus on how kids learned to smile and laugh.

'Both have their origins as expressions of fear or fright. Thus laughter begins when a baby is shocked by something – such as being lifted aloft by a playful parent. Within a nanosecond it discovers that it is not, after all, being threatened, that all is well, that it's going to survive. The lung full of air that was to provide a drawn out scream is, instead, employed in an explosive release of tension. The scream becomes a laugh, just as the gasp becomes a chuckle. And the smile, which began as a grimace of terror, softens as panic passes.'

In the adult, jokes are frequently little acts of exorcism – attempts to deal with fears and anxieties. We laugh about what we dislike, about what frightens us. Hence the abundance of jokes on sex, illness, politicians, foreigners, lawyers and old age. Adult jokes abound in bigotry and cynicism.

But what amuses kids? Having been shocked into smiling and laughing, is their humour as concerned with the human condition? Or does it reflect a more innocent experience of life? And if so, will that innocence long survive in a world of mass media – in which there are no secrets? It's becoming impossible to protect children from images of natural and man-made disasters, from images of war, accidental death and murder. Even if they can be deflected from watching or reading the news, their mass entertainment is increasingly violent.

It is our pleasant duty to report that, thus far, kids' humour remains childish, in both senses of the term. There is little evidence that it has become polluted or corrupted by the terrors of television or the horrors of Hollywood. Whilst emphatically earthy, involving a fascination with poo-poos and wee-wees (or whatever the approved term is in your family), the jokes are, by and large, amiable and nonsensical, sharing none of the nasties that amuse anxious adults. In fact, the words that children use to entertain themselves are, first and foremost, about words themselves. Children's jokes are expressions of delight in the very idea of language. Children like to play with words in the same way that they play with

Playdough or plasticine. The big, dark issues are put aside, awaiting the onset of puberty and, beyond that, maturity.

In the early teens, hormones begin the process of sexual blossoming. At more or less the right time the body will manufacture some powerful chemicals that will hit the appropriate receptors that will, in turn, produce a rising sap in the young of both sexes. With a delighted sense of gender, of sexuality, the pubescent child will start to suffer all the well advertised pangs, whilst at the same time, enjoying some unprecedented pleasures.

Something very similar happens with language.

If Noam Chomsky and his followers are right, language – the unique human ability to communicate an infinite variety of information and ideas through noises invented in the mouth – also begins with a specific hormone. At just the right time, a young human being begins to manufacture a chemical that, impacting on the brain, triggers the learning of any language to which the child is habitually exposed. No hormone – no language. Indeed, if the child hasn't learnt language between birth and puberty it will never learn to speak.

Chomsky's theories have been given substance by studies of feral children. Over the past few hundred years a number of children have turned up in human society who have apparently been raised by animals, or in inhuman conditions. Never having been exposed to language they tried to communicate by grunts and other simple noises. Whilst they can be taught a limited vocabulary of isolated words – so as to ask for food and drink – if they've passed the age of puberty they will never develop comprehensive language skills. The evidence suggests that they cannot, for the life of them, learn to grasp grammar or syntax. They will be unable to form even simple sentences. (About twenty years ago a feral child was discovered living in the suburbs of Los Angeles. She'd been locked in a room for most of her life, kept apart from other human beings and had no experience of speech. Once rescued it was possible to teach her a wide variety of human behaviour but language defeated her.)

What is impossible after puberty is a breeze for the very young. Once the hormone hits, words fill the mind and tumble from the mouth. The synapses crackle and the neurones oblige by storing a growing amount of information on both vocabulary and the structure of sentences. In fact, the human infant is primed to learn any language on earth. Chomsky demonstrates that all languages have an underlying structure, a similar mathematics to them, so that the baby will quickly become competent in Italian or Greek or Russian or Tagalog or Mandarin. And if it's living in a bilingual household it will learn both languages, at the same time, without the slightest effort. All in response to the detonation of a hormone.

Clearly children love language. The child is thrilled by its growing ability to use words. So he or she begins to play with them. To laugh with them. To laugh at them. Whatever else a child may play with – from blocks to dolls – words are the first play thing and remain the most popular.

As they thrill to their new skills in using words, they find them full of surprises and paradox. The same word can mean entirely different things – and there are jokes for that. Every child is an incipient Spike Milligan who likes to make puns and create surreal images. Indeed, the popularity of the *Goon Show* in the fifties is a testament to a child's tenacity. Milligan, like Edward Lear and Lewis Carroll before him, plays with words in a way that is at once innocent and sophisticated. He belongs to a great tradition of humourists who simply refuse to grow up.

What do cats read in the morning?
Mewspapers.

What do you call a duck with fangs?
Count Quackula.

How do you take a sick pig to hospital?
In a ham-bulance.

What goes zzub zzub zzub?
A bee flying backwards.

There are thousands of jokes like this – jokes in the ancient tradition of the riddle. Kids delight in such silliness. And they also enjoy repetition – hence the infinite numbers of knock knock jokes, where the words are given a uniformity of structure.

They delight in hearing old stories retold too – look at the durability of Cinderella against some pretty stiff competition from new technologies. And because kids are reassured by repetition they'll happily watch the same *Wallace and Gromit* video a hundred times. For all their delight and fascination with the new, they're also immensely comforted by the familiar.

When collecting adult jokes we discovered that overwhelmingly, jokes have ancient lineages. Old jokes are endlessly recycled, updated in setting and language. Thus a variety of jokes about Paul Keating turned out to have originated in Munich in the 1930s when the original target was Hitler. As well, adult jokes come rushing into the culture from films, novels and the Internet.

With kids, jokes are overwhelmingly traditional. Many, if not most of the jokes in this book will be painfully familiar to adults because they laughed at exactly the same jokes in kindergarten or primary school. Jokes are handed down from generation to generation like fairy stories and, yes, like nursery rhymes. An idiom will disappear for a time and then suddenly reappear in the playground – a bit like the game of marbles. It's as if children belong to a secret society full of rituals that must be protected and passed on. This is not to say that this secret society doesn't admit to new possibilities, to new traditions. You see that in the way a recent invention like the yo-yo can be added to the repertoire of marbles and hopscotch. And the same thing happens with humour.

Visiting schools – both State and multi-denominational – to gather this collection, we were astonished by the enthusiasm of the response. It wasn't necessary to beg kids or bribe them for contributions. Every hand in a class went up as kids competed for the opportunity to tell their favourites. And we could detect no significant difference between the sexes or various demographics. Kids all over Australia seem to be telling the same jokes at more or less the same time. If they weren't Irish jokes they were fatty and skinny jokes or elephant jokes.

Children live in a world where animals freely interact with human beings. A world of blind mice and eggs toppling off walls. Consequently, an overwhelming majority of jokes concern animals that talk or have traumatic experiences. Human beings play second fiddle to the menagerie – even parents, whom you'd expect to be dominant figures in kids' jokes, are few and far between. Perhaps that's why there was one particular joke that proved to be a marvellous ice-breaker. Trial and error showed that this was the one joke that all kids enjoyed. And perhaps it's an intimation of where jokes will, later, take them.

Why did the koala fall out of the tree? Because it was dead.

Simple, emphatic, no nonsense. The dead koala invariably provoked hilarity in the classroom. And the matter-of-factness of the joke defines another characteristic. 'Ask a silly question, get a simple answer.'

In that joke about the little furry creature subject to the dictates of gravity, we see perhaps the beginning of an ironic response to a world of growing dangers and difficulties. For finally that's what humour exists to do. To help you deal with life, in all its delights and difficulties.

The editors

Animal

Antics

'Who's the king of the jungle?' cried the lion to the zebra.

'You are, of course,' said the zebra shyly.

'Who's the king of the jungle?' asked the lion to the giraffe.

'Why you are dear lion,' said the giraffe.

'So who's the king of the jungle?' asked the lion to the elephant.

In an instant the elephant picked up the lion in its trunk and hurled him into the air.

'Now, now,' said the lion, 'no need to get nasty just because you don't know the answer!'

The Mummy and the baby camel were having a cuddle one day when the baby camel asked: 'Why do I have such long eyelashes?'

'Because they protect your eyes in a dust storm.'

'Why do I have such big feet?'

'So you won't sink in the sand my dear.'

'Why have I got such a big hump on my back?'

'So you can carry a large quantity of water when you're in the desert.'

'Well Mum, what am I doing in a zoo then?'

'I just ran into a great big bear!'
'Did you let him have both barrels?'
'Heavens no, I let him have the whole gun.'

What do you get if you cross a cocker spaniel, a poodle and a rooster?
Cockapoodledoo.

How did the skunk phone her mother?
On her smellular phone.

Where do steers party?
At the meat ball.

'If you see a leopard, shoot him on the spot!'
'OK, there's a leopard, now quick, which spot?'

What's the difference between a fish and a piano?
You can't tuna fish.

What do you call a bull that's sleeping?
A bull dozer.

What do you call a cow that doesn't give milk?
A milk dud.

What did the snake give his girlfriend on their first date?
A goodnight hiss.

What do cats put in their soft drink?
Mice cubes.

What goes wow wob?
A dog walking backwards.

What TV show is about investigating mysterious cattle?
'The Ox-Files.'

What do worms do in a cornfield?
They go in one ear and out the other.

What do you get when you cross a cow with a duck?
Milk and quackers.

The Queen has corgies, but what sort of cats does she have?
Aristocats.

Why did the farmer buy a brown cow?
Because he wanted chocolate milk.

If a snake and an undertaker were married, what would they inscribe on their towels?
Hiss and Hearse.

If you crossed a dog with a fax machine, what would you get?
A fax terrier.

What do they make at Telecow?
Moobile phones.

What do you call a cow with no legs?
Ground Beef.

What do you need to do if your chooks aren't laying?
Give them an eggs-ray.

Why do cats put mice in the freezer?
To make micey poles.

How does a dog stop a VCR?
He presses the paws button.

What's a cow's favourite TV show?
'Steer Trek.'

Where can you find the most cows?
Moo York.

What do you get from a nervous cow?
A milk shake.

What do you call a cold puppy sitting on a rabbit?
A chilli dog on a bun.

What's more fantastic than a talking dog?
A spelling bee.

What do you get if you cross a skunk with a bear?
Winnie the Pooh.

Where do jellyfish get their jelly from?
From ocean currants.

What do you get when you cross a dog with a hen?
Pooched eggs.

Why aren't turkeys ever invited to dinner parties?
Because they always use fowl language.

What do bees do with their honey?
They cell it.

What do you call a duck with fangs?
Count Quackula.

Where should you never go with a dog?
To the Flea Market.

What is a slug?
A snail with a housing problem.

What's black, white, smelly and noisy?
A skunk with a drum kit.

What did the dog say when he sat on sandpaper?
'Rough! Rough!'

Why did the girl keep tripping over lobsters?
Because she was accident prawn.

What goes zzub zzub zzub?
A bee flying backwards.

What do cats read in the morning?
Mewspapers.

'Has your cat ever had fleas?'
'No, but it's had kittens.'

What do you call a three-legged dog?
Skippy.

What animal always goes to bed with its shoes on?
A horse.

Why did the Dalmatian go to the cleaners?
His coat had spots all over it.

Why do dogs wag their tails?
Because no one will wag them for them.

What did Mr and Mrs Chicken call their baby?
Egg.

What's a dog's favourite fruit?
Paw paw.

Where do sheep do their shopping?
At Woolies.

Why did the dog tick?
Because it was a watchdog.

What has a coat all winter and pants in summer?
A dog.

'My father went hunting, and he shot three ducks.'
'Were they wild?'
'No, but the farmer who owned them was.'

What petrol do snails use?
Shell.

What do cows drink?
Cowpuccino.

Where do foxes go if they lose their tails?
To the retail shop.

What do you call a camel with three humps?
Humphrey.

What happens when a frog's car breaks down?
It gets toad away.

'My dog has no nose.'
'How does it smell?'
'Terrible.'

What do you call high-rise flats for pigs?
Sty scrapers.

Why did the man bring his dog to the railway station?
To train him.

How can you stop your dog barking in the hall?
Put him in the backyard.

Why did the two boaconstrictors get married?
Because they had a crush on each other.

Why did the lion spit out the clown?
Because he tasted funny.

What kind of tie does a pig wear?
A pigsty.

How do you spell 'mouse trap' using three letters?
C A T.

What sort of work do mice do?
Mousework.

What's a bear's favourite drink?
Ginger bear.

If a cat fell into a rubbish bin what would you call it?
Kitty litter.

What does an invisible cat drink?
Evaporated milk.

'Did you know it takes three sheep to make a jumper?'
'I didn't even know they could knit.'

Why do cats change their size?
Because they are let out at night and taken in in the morning.

What do pigs do after school?
Their hamwork.

What is long and slippery and goes 'hith'?
A snake with a lisp.

What do polar bears have for lunch?
Ice burgers.

What do you get when you cross a karate expert with a pig?
A pork chop.

'It's raining cats and dogs.'
'I know, I just stepped in a poodle.'

What do you call a travelling flea?
An itch hiker.

What do frozen cows do?
They give ice-cream.

What do you call a penguin in the desert?
Lost.

A very expensive dog is drowning in the river when a man jumps into the freezing water, swims over to the dog, brings it back to the shore, gives it mouth to mouth resuscitation and revives it. Meanwhile the dog's owner is running towards them having seen the whole episode.

'That was amazing, thank you so much. Are you a vet?'
'Of course I'm a vet, I'm absolutely soaking!'

'Ouch, I thought you said your dog didn't bite?'
'That's not my dog.'

What do you call a monkey with a banana in each ear?
Anything, because it can't hear you.

What did the echidna say to the cactus?
'Mummy!'

'My horse is a blacksmith.'
'What do you mean?'
'Well, if I shout at him, he makes a bolt for the door.'

What do you call a cow that eats your grass?
A lawn mooer.

What's worse than a giraffe with a sore throat?
A centipede with blisters.

What do you get when you stack toads together?
A toadempole.

Why do tigers eat raw meat?
Because they can't cook.

Why did the farmer name his pig 'ink'?
Because it kept running out of the pen.

What do you call a donkey with three legs?
A wonkey.

Why don't snakes have a sense of humour?
Because you can't pull their legs.

What goes oom oom oom?
A cow walking backwards.

Where do rabbits go after they get married?
On a bunny moon.

'Are you aware your dog barked all night?'
'Yes, but don't worry, he got plenty of sleep during the day.'

What does the buffalo say when he sends his son off to school each morning?
'Bison.'

What do you call one hundred rabbits jumping backwards?
A receding hare line.

What did the doctor prescribe for the bald rabbit?
Hare tonic.

What do you get when you pour hot water down a rabbit hole?
Hot cross bunnies.

Where do baby apes sleep?
In apricots.

What do cats eat at parties?
Mice cream.

What is a small turkey called?
A goblet.

Why do fish have such huge phone bills?
Because when they get on the line, they can't get off.

What is a squirrel's favourite ballet?
'The Nut Cracker Suite.'

What are the knees of baby goats called?
Kidneys.

What works in a circus and meows when it swings?
An acrocat.

What kind of key doesn't unlock any door?
A monkey.

What do you get when you cross a rabbit with a spider?
A hare net.

What's grey with a blue face?
A mouse holding its breath.

Why do cows wear bells?
Because their horns don't work.

How did the rodeo horse get so rich?
It had a lot of bucks.

Why don't fish go near computers?
They're afraid of getting caught in the Internet.

What did the rabbit give his girlfriend?
A five carrot ring.

How do you catch a squirrel?
Climb up a tree and act like a nut.

Which side of a chicken has the most feathers?
The outside.

Why is it easy to weigh fish?
Because they come with scales.

Why did the fox bang his head on the piano?
He was playing by ear.

Why did the kitten join the Red Cross?
Because it wanted to be a first aid kit.

What's a fish's favourite game show?
'Name that Tuna.'

Why do mother kangaroos hate rainy days?
Because their kids have to play inside.

What do you call a skunk in court?
Odour in the court.

Why did the crab go to jail?
Because it was always pinching things.

Why do bees buzz?
Because they can't whistle.

What are the most commonly used letters in the skunk alphabet?
'P' and 'U'.

What did the boy octopus say to the girl octopus?
'I want to hold your hand, hand, hand, hand, hand, hand, hand, hand.'

What mouse won't eat cheese?
A computer mouse.

Why couldn't the pony talk?
He was a little horse.

Where does a whale sleep?
On the sea bed.

What do you call a shy lamb?
Baaaashful.

Why do giraffes have such long necks?
Because their feet stink.

What do you get when you cross a snowball with a shark?
Frostbite.

How can you stop a rhinoceros from charging?
Take away its credit cards.

What should you do if you find a gorilla in your bed?
Find somewhere else to sleep.

What do you call an owl with a sore throat?
A bird that doesn't give a hoot.

When does a mouse need an umbrella?
When it's raining cats and dogs.

Why did the turtle cross the road?
To get to the shell station.

If chickens get up when the rooster crows, when do ducks get up?
At the quack of dawn.

What does a polar bear telephone operator say?
'Thank you, and have an ice day.'

What happened to the snake when it had a cold?
She adder viper nose.

Why shouldn't you play cards in the jungle?
Because there are too many cheetahs.

What did the little bird say when it found an orange in its nest?
'Look at the orange mama-laid!'

One cow said to the other: 'Are you worried about this mad cow disease?'
'No, why should I be? I'm a possum.'

What has six legs, bites, is noisy at night and talks in code?
A morse-quito.

What is the opposite of a cool cat?
A hot dog.

What does a snake learn when it goes to school?
Hiss-tory.

'Two of our chooks have stopped laying eggs.'
'How do you know?'
'Because I just ran over them with the tractor.'

How can you talk to a fish?
Drop it a line.

What animal can pray?
A praying mantis.

Why shouldn't you cry if a cow slips on the ice?
Because it's no use crying over spilt milk.

What's green and slimy and lives in my hanky?
My pet frog.

What's the difference between a buffalo and a bison?
You can't wash your hands in a buffalo.

What happened to the cat who ate a ball of wool?
She had mittens.

What animals on Noah's ark didn't come in pairs?
Worms. They came in apples.

Where do tadpoles change into frogs?
In the croakroom.

When is the best time to buy a budgie?
When they're going cheap.

What's a dog's favourite food?
Anything that's on your plate.

What do you get if you cross a rabbit and a sheep?
A Jumper.

What's a frog's favourite drink?
Croaka cola.

How do sheep keep warm in winter?
They turn on the central bleating.

Why did the chicken cross the road?
He saw a man laying bricks.

What do you call a duck that can't read?
A blind duck.

What is the sharpest pine?
A porcupine.

Why does the kookaburra laugh?
Because there's nothing to cry about.

Why did the chicken cross the football field?
Because the umpire cried foul.

What did the lion say when he saw two rabbits on a skateboard?
'Meals on wheels.'

Now you see it, now you don't, now you see it, now you don't. What is it?
A black cat on a zebra crossing.

What makes a dog meow?
A chainsaw. Meeeeeooooow!

Why do snakes have forked tongues?
Because they can't use chop sticks.

Why do gorillas live in the jungle?
Because they can't afford to live in the city.

How come koalas carry their babies on their backs?
They can't push a pram up a tree.

Two bats were out one night looking for blood, but after a few hours of unsuccessful hunting decided to go home. In the wee hours of the morning one of the bats was so hungry he said he had to go out hunting again. An hour later he came back all covered in blood.

'Where did you get that blood?' said the other bat full of envy.

'Come with me and I'll show you.' So out they went into the night.

'See that tree over there?' said the bat covered in blood.

'Yeah.'

'Well, I didn't!'

What's green and smells of eucalyptus?
Koala vomit.

Cow one: Moo.
Cow two: Baa Baa.
Cow one: What do you mean Baa Baa?
Cow two: I'm learning a second language.

What do you get if you sit under a cow?
A pat on the head.

How do goldfish go into business?
They start on a small scale.

'Hey! Your dog has just eaten my hat.'
'He'll be OK, he likes hats.'

What's a bear's second favourite drink?
Coca koala.

Two very big turtles and a very little turtle were sitting in a cafe drinking apple juice when it began to pour with rain. Since the little turtle was the quickest they decided that he should go back home and get their raincoats. But the little one objected. He was worried that when he left, the others would drink his apple juice. It took a lot of convincing, but finally, he was persuaded to head off for the raincoats. Three weeks later one of the big turtles said: 'Let's drink his juice.'

'I'd been thinking exactly the same thing,' said the other.

And from just a few yards away, on the footpath, a little voice said: 'Oh no you don't. If you do, I won't go home and get the raincoats.'

Where do you find the biggest spider?
In the World Wide Web.

Why did the chicken cross the playground?
To get to the other slide.

What happened to the two bedbugs who fell in love?
They got married in the spring.

What does a toad say when it sees something wonderful?
'Toad-ally awesome.'

What kind of shoes does a toad wear?
Open toad sandals.

What are spider webs good for?
Spiders.

Why does a polar bear have fur?
Because it would look silly in leather.

Two men were walking along Bondi early one morning with a shaggy dog. The dog's owner threw the stick into the ocean and the dog ran across the top of the water, collected the stick and bought it back. The other man couldn't believe his eyes.

'That is one amazing dog you have there,' said the man.

'Amazing my foot,' said the dog's owner. 'After all the lessons he's had he still can't swim.'

Who went into the lion's den and came out alive?
The lion.

What do ants take when they are sick?
Antibiotics.

What game do hogs play?
Pig pong.

Where do you find rabbits in Paris?
They're in the hutch, at the back of Notre Dame.

Baby snake: My head hurts.
Mummy snake: Come here and let me hiss it.

'My dog's head is always hanging down so I'm taking him to the vet's.'
'Neck's weak?'
'No, tomorrow.'

'I knew someone who thought he was an owl.'
'Who?'
'Make that two people.'

Why was Mummy centipede so upset?
All the kids needed new shoes.

What did the mother bee say to the naughty baby bee?
'Beehive yourself.'

Why do bees itch?
Because they have hives.

What did the mother glow worm say to the father glow worm?
'Wow, our baby sure is bright.'

Where do you take sick kangaroos?
To the hop-ital.

Where do you take sick dogs?
To the dog-tor.

How do you take sick pigs to the hospital?
In a ham-bulance.

How many toes does a monkey have?
Take off your shoes and count them.

Why don't monkeys live on the moon?
Because there aren't any bananas there.

What is every cat's favourite nursery rhyme?
'Three Blind Mice.'

Why does a dog sit on its hind legs?
If it didn't it would be standing up.

How do baby hens dance?
Chick to chick.

Why did the ibis cross the road?
To prove it wasn't chicken.

'Have you got any dogs going cheap?'
'No, all my dogs go "woof".'

What do you call a good looking emu?
Rare.

Where do you find a tortoise with no legs?
Where you left it.

What does a frog drink when he's on a diet?
Diet croak.

How many monkeys does it take to change a light globe?
Two. One to do it, and one to scratch his bottom.

A man goes into a shop with a pig under his arm. The manager spots him and says:
'That's the ugliest looking animal you've got there. Where on earth did you get it?'
   And the pig says, 'I won it in a raffle.'

What year do frogs like the best?
Leap year.

One morning Daddy Bear came down to breakfast to find his porridge bowl empty.

'Somebody's been eating my porridge,' said Daddy Bear.

'And somebody's been eating my porridge,' said Baby Bear.

At that moment Mummy Bear came out of the kitchen and said: 'You silly bears. I haven't made it yet!'

Which birds are religious?
Birds of prey.

Why did the farmer light a fire next to his goat?
Because he wanted to boil his billy.

What bird is a good cook?
A kookaburra.

What kind of cat is found in a library?
A catalogue.

What do you call a bird with a cold?
A cocka choo.

What's the hardest part about milking a mouse?
Getting a bucket under it.

What bird can't you trust?
A lyrebird.

What's a cat's favourite holiday destination?
The Canary Islands.

'I don't like these flies buzzing around me!'
'Well, pick out the ones you like and I'll try to get rid of the rest.'

One flea says to the other as he walks down the road: 'Shall we keep on walking or catch a dog?'

'I want that bird!'
'It's all yours Madam, but it costs twenty dollars.'
'Will you send me the bill?'
'No, you have to take the whole bird.'

I saw a bird up in the sky,
Who dropped a message from up high,
As I wiped it from my eye,
I thanked the Lord that cows don't fly.

Why do bees have sticky hair?
Because they use honey combs.

What did the mosquito say the first time it saw the camel's hump?
'Did I do that?'

Why didn't the butterfly go to the dance?
Because it was a mothball.

What do frogs sit on?
Toadstools.

Where do wasps go when they're sick?
To waspital.

What do you call a mosquito that likes cheese?
A mozzie-rella.

Why were two flies playing football on a saucer?
Because they were practising for the cup.

What lays around 100 feet up?
A dead centipede.

Why does a dog turn around twice before sitting down?
Because one good turn deserves another.

Where do frogs keep their money?
In the riverbank.

'Does your dog have a licence?'
'No, he isn't old enough to drive.'

What did the spaniel say to the bird?
'I'm a cocker too.'

Why do birds fly north?
Because it's too far to walk.

Do cows give milk?
No, you have to take it from them.

Three bees decided to build a car. One worked on the motor, the second on the body and the third on the upholstery. Finally they completed the task and were very proud of themselves. All they needed was some petrol and they could have their first drive.

Whereupon a grasshopper arrived and asked: 'Can I help?'

'Sorry,' chorused the bees. 'This car only takes BP.'

What kind of horses go out at night?
Night mares.

What goes through a grasshopper's mind when it hits the windscreen of a car going at 100 kilometres per hour?
Its legs.

Why do bees hum?
Because they don't know the words.

What do you get when you cross a black sheep with a bra?
'Bra Bra Black Sheep.'

What's the best way to keep a dog off the street?
Keep it in a barking lot.

What did the rat do when his girlfriend fell into the dam?
He gave her mouse to mouse resuscitation.

Why are fish poor tennis players?
Because they don't like to get close to the net.

Why are fish smart?
Because they always go to school.

What did the duck say when she finished shopping?
'Just put it on my bill.'

What kind of shoes are made of banana skins?
Slippers.

How do you catch a runaway dog?
Make a noise like a bone.

What did the pig say when the farmer got hold of his tail?
'That's the end of me!'

What did Mrs Spider say to Mr Spider when he broke her new web?
'Darn it!'

Why is it hard to have a conversation with a goat around?
Because it always butts in.

Why couldn't the leopard escape from the zoo?
Because he was always spotted.

If ten cats were on a boat and one jumped out, how many would be left?
None, they were all copycats.

Why did the three little pigs leave home?
Because their father was a crashing boar.

Why does a monkey scratch itself?
Nobody else knows where it itches.

What horse never wears a saddle?
A seahorse.

Where do you find dinosaurs?
It depends where you leave them.

If horses wear horse shoes, what do camels wear?
Desert boots.

What kind of horse can become a head of a council?
A mare.

What horse can give you a cold?
A draught horse.

'My dog's missing.'
'Put an ad in the paper.'
'But dogs can't read!'

If a man has a dog with no legs what can he do?
Take him for a drag!

How do you find your lost dog in the Botanical Gardens?
Put your ear to a tree and listen to the bark.

What dog never barks?
A hot dog.

What do you get when you cross a bear and a kangaroo?
A fur coat with big pockets.

What did the farmer put on the pig's sore nose?
Oinkment.

What type of shoes do koalas wear?
Gum boots.

What do you get when you cross a pig with a car?
Another kind of crashing boar.

Where do you find wombats?
It depends where they are lost.

Why is a bilby like a one cent piece?
Because it has a head one end and a tail on the other.

What can you do with a short-sighted kangaroo?
Get it to a hop-tician.

A young woman was out bush walking when she came across a friendly wombat on the side of the road. She picked it up and took it to a police station.

'What should I do with this?' she asked the policeman.

'Take him to the zoo,' he replied.

The next morning the policeman saw the woman with the wombat again.

'I thought I told you to take it to the zoo?'

'I did, and this afternoon we're going to the movies.'

How many animals can you put in an empty cage?
One. After that it is not empty.

What do cows eat for breakfast?
Mooslie.

What did the shopkeeper say to the cow?
'Do you want this one or the udder?'

Why did the koala fall out of the tree?
Because it was dead.

What sort of lollies do koalas eat?
Chewing gum.

What's a horse after it's six months old?
Seven months old.

What do you get if a sheep studies karate?
Lamb chops.

What did the rabbit say to the carrot?
'It's been nice gnawing you.'

What's green, red, disgusting and makes a gluggy noise?
A frog in the blender.

What does a giraffe have that no other animals have?
Baby giraffes.

When is it OK to drink rhinoceros milk?
When you're a baby rhinoceros.

Where was the donkey when the light went out?
In the dark.

What's a horse's favourite TV show?
'Neighbours.'

What do you get when you cross a sheep and a kangaroo?
A woolly jumper.

What can you do when a tiger eats your dictionary?
Take the words out of its mouth.

How do you know when you have a hundred wombats trying to get into your fridge?
You can't shut the door.

Why don't kangaroos ride bikes?
Because they don't have a thumb to ring the bell.

Why did the cow jump over the moon?
Because the farmer had cold hands.

Why did the dinosaur cross the road?
Because the chicken hadn't been invented yet.

Why did the bee cross his legs?
Because he couldn't find the BP Station.

What kind of animal can jump higher than a house?
All kinds because houses can't jump.

What do you get if you cross a rabbit with a bumble bee?
A honey bunny.

Dingdong bell,
Pussy's in the well.
If you don't believe me,
Go and have a smell.

What do you call a mouse if you put it in the freezer?
Mice.

Why do wombats dig with their claws?
Because they can't use bulldozers.

How can you tell if a bee is on the phone?
You get a busy signal.

'Sally, have you given the goldfish fresh water today?'
'No, they haven't finished the water they had yesterday.'

Johnny went into the cafe to order a milkshake for himself and a diet soda for his pet giraffe. Soon after they finished their drinks, the giraffe fell off its chair and dropped dead. A man walked in and stared at the dead animal and said: 'What's that lying on the floor?'

'Don't be stupid, that's not a lion. It's a giraffe,' said Johnny.

There are three dogs and three men, and they have to get across the desert without the dogs making a mess. The first man gets a quarter of the way across when, unfortunately, his dog does a poo. The second man gets halfway when his dog also does a poo. But the last man gets all the way. How did he do it?

'Me not silly, me not dumb, me shove cork up doggy's bum.'

An old man is walking along the street when he sees a frog. The frog says: 'Hey, mate, come over here.' The old man walks over and the frog says: 'Pick me up.' So the old man picks up the frog. The frog says: 'If you rub me, I'll turn into a genie and give you lots of money.' The old man puts the frog in his pocket and starts to walk on. The frog squirms and wiggles and yells: 'Hey, take me out of your pocket!' So the old man takes him out of his pocket. The frog stares at the man and shouts: 'I said, I'd turn into a genie and give you whatever you wanted!'

To this the old man replied: 'Look, at my age, I'd rather have a talking frog!'

Which animal is best at cricket?
A bat.

What did the cat have for breakfast?
Mice crispies.

What sort of fish go meow?
Catfish.

What should you do if you find a snake in your bed?
Sleep somewhere else.

How does an octopus go to war?
Well armed.

What do you get when you put a Tasmanian devil into a chicken coop?
Devilled eggs.

Where are you most likely to see a man-eating fish?
In a seafood restaurant.

What did the fish say to the seaweed?
'Kelp, Kelp!'

'Have you ever hunted bear?'
'No, but I've been fishing in my shorts.'

Why did Little Bo-Peep lose her sheep?
Because she had a crook with her.

What kind of cat helps you fix things?
A tool kit.

In what book do ducks look up words?
A duck-tionary.

What gives milk, goes moo and makes all your wishes come true?
Your dairy godmother.

How do you move cows?
In a moo-ving van.

What kind of cow can you sit on?
A cow-ch.

Why was the sheep arrested on the dual carriageway?
Because he did a ewe turn.

What dance do you get if you cross a fox and a horse?
The fox trot.

What's the easiest way to count cows?
On a cow-culator.

Where do sheep go for their holidays.
To the Baa Haa Maa's.

Which singer do cows prefer?
Moodonna.

What type of underwear do zebras wear?
Z-bra.

What do pigs wear to bed?
Pig-jamas.

What's a lion's favourite dance?
Lion-dancing.

What's a monkey's favourite dance?
The orang-a-tango.

How do rabbits travel?
By hare-plane.

What's an octopus's favourite lolly?
A jelly bean.

Why did the dog have to go to court?
Because he got a barking ticket.

'Did you ever see a catfish?'
'Don't be mad. Cats don't fish.'

What do you get when you cross a rooster with a steer?
A cock and bull story.

What do you get if you cross a giraffe with a hedgehog?
A ten metre toothbrush.

How many skunks does it take to stink out a room?
A phew.

What kind of fish do they serve on airplanes?
Flying fish.

Family Life

'Darling,' said the pregnant woman, 'I know how excited you are about becoming a father, but I have to tell you something. In my family we have a tradition that the wife's brother always gets to name the children. I was too nervous to tell you before, but it just has to be that way.'

'But your brother is a complete idiot,' said the husband, 'he'll make a mess of it.'

A little later, beautiful, healthy twins were born. A boy and a girl. So the father asked his wife what names her brother had chosen for his children.

'Well, the girl is Denise,' the mother said quietly.

'That's a pretty name. Perhaps this won't be so bad after all. And what's our son's name?'

'Denephew.'

'Mum, I'm tired of looking like everyone else, could you part my hair from ear to ear please?'

'Are you sure?'

'Yeah.'

That day Johnny came home from school really depressed.

'Can you do my hair back the other way again Mum?'

'What's the matter Johnny, are you sick of being different already?'

'It's not that, I can't stand people whispering in my nose.'

'Now little Mary eat your greens up, or you won't grow up to be beautiful!'

'Nanna, didn't you eat your greens?'

'Mum, can I have a dollar for the man who's crying in the park?'
'What's he crying about?'
He's crying, "Hot dogs, one dollar!"'

How did the farmer mend his pants?
With cabbage patches.

'What are you doing there Johnny, digging that hole?'
'I'm burying my radio. The batteries are dead.'

'Johnny, why have you put sugar in your pillow?'
'So I'll have sweet dreams, Mum.'

'Johnny, why aren't you playing tennis with Simon any more?'
'Mum, would you play with someone who always lies about the score?'
'Absolutely not.'
'Well, neither would Simon!'

'Polly, take that hose out of Johnny's ear!'
'But I'm trying to brainwash him.'

'Daddy, Daddy, can I have another glass of water please?'
'You've already had eight.'
'Yes, but my bedroom's on fire!'

'Johnny, you can't take that sweet to the dentist's appointment!'
'Why not, I want a chocolate filling.'

What do fairy children do when they get home from school?
Their gnome work.

'Johnny, it's time to get up. It's five to eight.'
'Who's winning?'

'Get your father out of that fridge!'
'But I want a cool pop, Mum.'

'Johnny, I think your dog really likes me, he hasn't taken his eyes off me all night.'
'That's because you're eating off his plate.'

Why did Nanna have roller blades fitted to her wheelchair?
So she could rock and roll.

'Johnny, I've told you not to let Rover into the house. It's full of fleas.'
'Rover, you keep out of the house, it's full of fleas.'

'Why is your baby so full of joy?'
'Because she's full of nappiness.'

'Dad, why have you painted rabbits on your head?'
'Can you tell? I thought from a distance they'd look like hares.'

'Dad, I'm really homesick.'
'But this is your home.'
'I know, I'm sick of it.'

'Dad, what did the X-ray of your brain show?'
'Uh, nothing much, son.'

Mum and Dad decided to take all their relatives out to dinner.
Both Mum and Dad ordered a mixed grill. 'And what about your vegetables?' asked the waiter.
'Oh, they can order what they like!' said Dad.

'Johnny, why did you sleep last night with a ruler?'
'Because I wanted to see how long I slept, Mum!'

'Johnny, you are disgusting, why do you pick your nose?'
'Because I can Mum.'

'You're an actor right?'
'Yeah.'
'Well how much will you charge to dress up as a ghost and scare my brother?'
'For $100, I'll scare him out of his wits.'
'Here's $50, he's only a half wit.'

'Mum, I have to write an essay on the High Court.'
'Well that's going to be difficult, paper would be much easier.'

'Johnny, you've got your shoes on the wrong feet again.'
'But they're the only feet I've got!'

'Daddy, can you see any change in me?'
'No, why son?'
'Because I just swallowed twenty cents.'

'Mum, I want to learn to play the piano by ear.'
'Well it's much easier if you use your hands.'

'Johnny, that essay you wrote about your dog is exactly the same as your sister's.'
'Of course teacher, it's the same dog.'

'Teacher, my Dad said there were three kinds of people in the world, those who can count and those who can't.'

'Johnny, did you put the cat out?'
'Why? Was it on fire?'

'Mum, can I swim on a full stomach?'
'No Johnny, it's better to swim on water.'

'Mum, why isn't my nose twelve inches long?'
'Because then it would be a foot.'

'Dad, a man came to see you this afternoon.'
'Did he have a bill?'
'No. He had a nose like yours.'

'Johnny, how are you enjoying your new guitar?'
'I threw it away Dad. It had a hole in the middle.'

Why did Johnny wear wet trousers?
Because the label said wash and wear.

'Why are you jumping up and down Johnny?'
'I took my medicine, but I forgot to shake the bottle.'

'Dad, have your socks got holes in them?'
'Certainly not, Johnny.'
'Well, how do you get your feet in them?'

'Johnny, which month has twenty-eight days?'
'They all have, Miss.'

'Dad, there's a man at the door collecting for a new swimming pool.'
'Give him a glass of water son.'

'My Dad owns a newspaper.'
'Yeah? He must be rich.'
'Not really. He bought it at the newsagent this morning.'

'My Dad can hold up a car with one hand.'
'Yeah? He must be really strong.'
'No. He's a policeman.'

'Mum, are we poisonous snakes?'
'No, of course not.'
'Just as well, because I just bit my lip.'

'Dad, are you still growing?'
'No, why do you ask?'
'Because your head is growing through your hair.'

'Mum, how can I get rid of my BO?'
'Hold your nose.'

'Mum, what has a purple spotted body, ten hairy legs, and big eyes on stalks?'
'I don't know.'
'Well, one just crawled up your dress.'

What's brown, hairy and has no legs but walks?
Dad's socks.

Little Belinda is playing with her mother's purse, pulls out all the coins and swallows one. Mum and Dad rush her to hospital.
 'How is our precious little daughter?'
 'Not much change yet,' says the nurse.

Mum and Dad go to dinner at the local

restaurant. Dad's halfway through his meal when he has a long, hard look at the potato. He calls the waitress over and says: 'This potato is bad.'

The waitress picks it up, smacks it, and puts it back on the plate.

'Now, if that potato gives you any more trouble, just let me know.'

When is a mummy not a mummy?
When it's a daddy.

'Dad, have you ever seen an oil well?'
'Why, no son I haven't. But I haven't seen one sick either.'

'Look out son! There's a ten foot snake behind you!'
'You can't fool me Dad. Snakes don't have feet.'

'Wow, your microscope magnifies three times.'
'Oh no! I've already used it twice.'

'Could I get a puppy for my son?'
'No Madam, we don't swap.'

Mum and Dad were driving in the country when they realised they were desperate for a cup of tea. Finally they arrived at a small town with a cafe. They pulled up, went inside and were just about to order when a horse walked in and sat at the table next to them. To their astonishment the horse ordered a coffee. Dad was so surprised that he asked the waitress if it was normal.

'No, he usually orders a lemonade!' she said.

Why do little brothers chew with their mouths open?
Flies have got to live somewhere.

'Hey Sis, what's that brain sucker doing on your head wasting its time?'

'Where does your sister live?'
'Alaska.'
'Don't worry, I'll ask her myself.'

'What's small, annoying and really ugly?'
'I'm not sure, but it comes when I call out my little sister's name.'

'Darling, what do you think? I just got back from the beauty parlour.'
'Too bad it was closed.'

Why did the parents call both their sons Jonathan?
Because two Jonathans are better than one.

When do you put a frog in your sister's bed?
When you can't catch a mouse.

What's grey, wrinkled and hangs out your underwear?
Your Grandma.

'Mum, can I have a parrot for Christmas?'
'No, you'll have turkey like the rest of us.'

Johnny came home with one thong.
'Did you lose a thong again?'
'No, I found one.'

Johnny and Mary are sitting on the beach playing with their navels.

'What are these?'

'Well, when you're born there's a piece of rope hanging out of there. They cut it off and twist the end around and tape it inside.'

'What for?'

'So you won't go pssssshhhhh and go down.'

Little Johnny was six and still hadn't spoken a word. Finally, one morning at breakfast he cried out, 'Mum, the toast's burnt!' His amazed mother gave him a big kiss and hug and asked: 'Johnny, why haven't you ever spoken before?'

'Well, up until now everything was fine.'

I've got five noses, seven mouths and six ears, so what am I?
Really ugly.

What goes up on your birthday but never comes down?
Your age.

Husband: Darling, there's a fat hairy ugly thing on your neck!
Wife: Where?
Husband: Oh don't worry, it's just your head.

'Mummy, Mummy, the kids at school say I look like a werewolf.'
'Shut up son and comb your face.'

What did the girl say to her Grandfather when he was drowning?
'Paddle Pop!'

'My nose keeps growing.'
'Stop telling so many lies then.'
'I never tell lies.'
'There it goes again.'

'Johnny, what time is it please, it must be after midnight?'
'I don't know Mum, my watch only goes to twelve.'

'Johnny, I'm sorry to have to tell you this, but we had to shoot Rover today.'
'Was he mad?'
'Well he wasn't too happy about it.'

A little boy kept wiping his nose on his sleeve, when another boy came up and asked: 'Haven't you got a hankie?'

'Yeah, but I don't think my Mum would like me to lend it to anyone.'

Fatty & Skinny

Fatty and Skinny climbed a tree,
Fatty fell down the lavatory.
Skinny went down to pull the chain,
And Fatty was never seen again.

Fatty was on the dunny.
Skinny was in the bath,
Fatty let off a fart,
and made poor Skinny laugh.

Fatty and Skinny went to bed,
Fatty rolled over and Skinny was dead.

Fatty and Skinny had a car.
Fatty had the crash. And Skinny had the scar.

Fatty and Skinny went to Mars,
Fatty came back with lots of bras.

Fatty and Skinny climbed up a tree,
Fatty got sick and did a big pee.

Fatty and Skinny went to the zoo,
Fatty stepped in elephant's poo.
Skinny went home to tell his Mum,
And all he got was a kick up the bum.

Fatty and Skinny went to the movies,
Skinny got excited when he saw some boobies.

Food Glorious Food

The gourmet food contest was underway and each chef was explaining their recipes.
'I use exactly 239 beans in my taco mix, one more and it would be too farty,' said the Mexican cook.

What's worse than finding a worm in your apple?
Half a worm.

What's the difference between a soft drink and a glass of water?
About a dollar twenty.

What kind of bean will never grow in a vegetable garden?
A jelly bean.

Why won't you ever be hungry at the beach?
Because of all the sand-which-is there.

Where do vegetables take their rusty cars for a service?
To the car-rot station.

Ummm, I like kids, but I don't think I could eat a whole one.

What is a potato's favourite TV show?
'MASH.'

A sandwich walks into a cafe and says: 'Hey, can I have a milkshake?'
   The waitress says: 'Sorry mate, we don't serve food here.'

How do you mend a broken pizza?
With tomato paste.

Baby corn: Where did I come from, Mum?
Mummy corn: The stalk brought you.

What's yellow, brown and hairy?
Cheese on toast, dropped on the carpet.

Why should potatoes grow better than any other vegetable?
Because they have eyes and can see what they're doing.

What day do chickens hate the most?
Fry days.

Why were the baby apricots crying?
Because their mummy was in the jam.

What kind of vegetable do they make
Lassie's dog biscuits with?
Collie-flour.

Why did the apple turn over?
Because it saw the swiss roll.

What kind of food do scarecrows like?
Strawberries.

Why did the biscuit go to the hospital?
Because he was feeling crummy.

Where were potatoes first fried?
In Greece.

What's in Paris, and is really high and wobbly?
The trifle tower.

Which vegetable is good at snooker?
A cue-cumber.

What do you get when you cross a potato with an onion?
A potato with watery eyes.

What kind of apple isn't an apple?
A pineapple.

Why didn't the duck eat his soup?
He couldn't find his quackers.

If I had six grapefruit in one hand and seven in the other, what would I have?
Very big hands.

What's red and green?
A tomato working part-time as a cucumber.

Why do skeletons drink milk?
Because it's good for their bones.

What do hungry stars do?
Chew on the Milky Way.

What kind of cheese comes with a house?
Cottage cheese.

Where does Superman buy his groceries?
At the supermarket of course.

Why did the chicken lay the egg?
Because if she dropped it it would break.

'Have you seen the salad bowl?'
'No, but I've seen the lunch box.'

What did the mayonnaise say to the refrigerator door?
'Shut the door, I'm dressing.'

How do you help deaf oranges?
Give them a lemon aid.

Should you eat your soup with your right or left hand?
Neither, you should use a spoon.

Why should you never tell secrets in a greengrocers?
Because potatoes have eyes and beans talk.

Why did the egg go to the jungle?
Because it was an eggs-plorer.

A peanut sat on the railway track,
His heart was all a flutter.
The five fifteen came rushing by,
'toot! toot!'
Peanut butter!

How do you make an artichoke?
Strangle it.

What vegetable has a heart in its head?
A lettuce.

What do traffic wardens have in their sandwiches?
Traffic jam.

If you were locked in a room with only a calendar and a bed, how could you survive?
You could eat the dates from the calendar and drink from the springs in the bed.

'Dad, I just can't work on an empty stomach!'
'Well, try the table then!'

'Why are you dancing with that jar of honey?'
'It says "Twist to open".'

What did the tomato say to his friend who was running behind him?
'Ketch-up!'

Why did the peanut go to the police?
Because it had been assalted.

What do you call a train full of toffee?
A chew chew train.

What stays hot in the refrigerator?
Mustard.

There was a young lady from Surrey,
Who cooked up a large pot of curry.
She ate the whole lot,
Straight from the pot,
And ran to the tap in a hurry.

What did the mother cabbage say to her son when he told a lie?
'You better turn over a new leaf.'

What do you call two rows of vegetables?
A dual cabbageway.

Why did twelve people walk out of the cafe at the same time?
Because they had all finished eating.

What do eskimos eat for breakfast?
Ice Krispies.

What has bread on both sides and is scared of everything?
A chicken sandwich.

What nuts can be found in space?
Astronuts.

How do you make a sausage roll?
Push it down the hill.

How do you make an apple puff?
Chase it around the garden.

Why did the steak feel suffocated?
Because it was smothered in onions.

Why did the biscuit cry?
Because his mother had been a wafer so long.

Why did the banana go to the doctor?
Because it wasn't peeling very well.

What should a prize fighter drink?
Punch.

What do you get when you cross a hairy monster and a dozen eggs?
A very hairy omelette.

What's white, fluffy and lives in the jungle?
A meringue-utan.

What do you get if you feed a chicken whisky?
Scotch eggs.

What is small, round and giggles a lot?
A tickled onion.

What's the hardest thing in the world to do?
Milk arrowroot biscuits.

What is wrapped in gladwrap and lives in a bell tower?
The lunch pack of Notre Dame.

What looks like half a loaf of bread?
The other half.

What type of bread is the best for an actor?
A large roll.

What do you call a mushroom who makes you laugh all day?
A fun-gi to be with.

Why is watermelon filled with water?
Because it's planted in the spring.

Why did the banana go out with the prune?
Because it couldn't find a date.

What's a monster's favourite soup?
Scream of tomato.

What's the best time to eat lunch?
After breakfast and before tea.

What kind of flower can you eat?
Forget-me-nuts.

What's the difference between a soldier and a fireman?
You can't dip a fireman in your boiled egg.

What's the difference between a banana and a tiger?
It takes ages to peel a tiger.

What do you call a thief who only steals meat?
A hamburglar.

What did one melon say to the other melon on St Valentine's day?
'Honeydew, I do love you!'

What do cavemen eat for lunch?
Club sandwiches.

What nut is like a sneeze?
A cashew.

What is the strongest vegetable?
A muscle sprout.

What do space aliens eat for breakfast?
Flying sausages.

What do astronauts put in their sandwiches?
Launch meat.

What did one kitchen knife say to the other kitchen knife?
'You're looking sharp today.'

What vegetable can draw water from a well?
A pump-kin.

What tastes hot but always has ice in it?
Spice.

What is bad tempered and goes with custard?
Apple grumble.

What makes the Tower of Pisa lean?
It doesn't eat.

What do you call a robbery in Beijing?
A Chinese takeaway.

Why don't bananas use sunscreen?
So they can peel more easily.

What do ghosts eat with meat?
Grave-y.

What makes suits and eats spinach?
Popeye the Tailorman.

What did the astronaut see in his frying pan?
An unidentified frying object.

What do you get when a monster steps on a house?
Mushed rooms.

What do you get from an educated oyster?
Pearls of wisdom.

Why did the lettuce close its eyes?
Because it didn't want to see the salad dressing.

What letter of the alphabet makes pies sneaky?
'S'. Because it turns pies into spies.

What would you get if you crossed a book of nursery rhymes with an orange?
Tales of Mother Juice.

What do you call a carrot who talked back to the farmer?
A fresh vegetable.

'There is no chicken in this chicken pie.'
'Well do you expect to find dogs in dog biscuits?'

'And how did you find your steak?'
'It wasn't hard, it was just between the potato and the peas.'

'Waiter, waiter, I'm in a hurry, will my pizza be long?'
'No, it will be round.'

'Waiter, waiter, there's a spider in my soup, get me the manager!'
'He won't come, he's scared of them too.'

'Waiter, waiter, this soup tastes funny!'
'Then why aren't you laughing?'

'Waiter, waiter, do you serve crabs in this restaurant?'
'We serve anyone, please take a seat.'

'Waiter, waiter, this apple pie is squashed!'
'You told me to step on it sir because you were in a hurry.'

'Waiter, waiter, how long will my sausages be?'
'Oh, about four inches sir.'

'Waiter, waiter, do you have frog's legs?'
'No, sir, I've always walked like this.'

'Waiter, waiter, there's a button on my plate!'
'I'm sorry sir, it must have fallen off the jacket potato.'

'Waiter, waiter, there's a button in my soup!'
'It must have come off while the salad was dressing.'

'Waiter, waiter, there's a dead fly in my soup!'
'Yes sir, the hot water killed it.'

'Waiter, waiter, what's this?'
'It's called a tomato surprise.'
'I can't see any tomatoes.'
'Yes, that's the surprise.'

'Waiter, waiter, this coffee tastes of mud!'
'That's right, it was only ground this morning.'

'Waiter, waiter, this soup is full of toadstools!'
'I know sir, there wasn't mushroom for anything else.'

'Waiter, waiter, I need something to eat and make it snappy!'
'How about a crocodile sandwich?'

'Waiter, waiter, what is wrong with this fish?'
'Long time, no sea, sir.'

'Waiter, waiter, there are holes in my cheese!'
'Just eat the cheese and leave the holes.'

'Waiter, waiter, there's a small slug on my plate!'
'Wait a minute, I'll try and get you a bigger one.'

'Waiter, waiter, you've got your finger on my steak.'
'Well, I didn't want it to drop on the floor again.'

'Waiter, waiter, there's a twig in my soup.'
'Yes, we have branches everywhere.'

'Waiter, waiter, this egg is bad.'
'Don't blame me, I only laid the table.'

What is the hottest letter in the alphabet?
'B'. Because it makes oil, boil.

What did the egg say to the dinosaur?
'You're egg-stinct.'

'Go over and trip that waiter, and we'll see some flying saucers.'

What turns without moving?
Milk, it can turn sour.

What goes up in the air white and comes down yellow and white?
An egg.

What animal hides in a grape?
An ape.

What's a hedgehog's favourite food?
Prickled onions.

Why did the orange stop rolling down a hill?
Because it ran out of juice.

What letter of the alphabet can make a plum fatter?
'P'. Because it makes plum, plump.

'Eat your cabbage up Johnny, it will put colour in your cheeks!'
'But I don't want green cheeks Mum.'

What do you call a biscuit that's good at school?
A smart cookie.

How do oceans cook?
In micro waves.

What do you call a rich fish?
A goldfish.

Why is this bread full of holes?
Because it's wholemeal bread.

Why did the potato cry?
Because the chips were down.

What is bright orange and sounds like a parrot?
A carrot.

What vegetable is like a chicken farm?
An egg-plant.

Why did the baker stop making doughnuts?
Because he got tired of the hole business.

What did Mary have when she went out to dinner?
Every one knows Mary had a little lamb.

What do thieves eat?
Takeaway.

What is golden brown, flat, has maple syrup on it, and doesn't want to grow up.
Peter Pancake.

What do you call an angry chocolate bar?
A violent crumble.

What do you call a chocolate easter bunny that has stayed in the sun too long?
A runny bunny.

What pies can fly?
Magpies.

What's the best thing to put into a pie?
Your teeth.

What did the older egg say to the younger egg?
'Life is a great egg-sperience.'

What's an egg that does gymnastics?
An egg flip.

What do you call a silly egg?
An egg-nog.

What do you call an egg that knows everything?
An eggs-pert.

What made the biscuit box?
It saw the fruit punch.

What starts out as batter and ends up flattened?
A pancake.

What did one egg say to another?
'You're cracked.'

What did the horse say when he had nothing else left to eat in the paddock but thistle?
'Thistle have to do!'

Why did the cucumber need a lawyer?
Because it was in a pickle.

Why did the strawberry need a lawyer?
Because it was in a jam.

What sweet does Jaws like best?
Shark-o-late.

What happened to the very bad egg?
It was egg-secuted.

What did the egg say to the blender?
'I know when I'm beaten.'

Which birds are on every person's meal?
Swallows.

What do you get if you cross a cat with a lemon?
A sour puss.

What do you call a pig in a restaurant?
A pig out.

What do you call a Grandma banana?
Nana.

A piece of bacon and a sausage are in the frying pan being cooked. The sausage says: 'It's hot in here isn't it?'
  And the bacon replied: 'Wow! A talking sausage.'

Why can any hamburger run a mile under four minutes?
Because it is fast food.

Why did the orange cross the road?
Because he wanted to show his girlfriend how to play squash.

How do you make Holy water?
You burn the Hell out of it.

What did the apple tree say to the farmer?
Stop picking on me.

What's the most dangerous vegetable on a ship?
A leek.

What tables are cooked and eaten?
Vegetables.

What can you serve but not eat?
A tennis ball.

Why did the banana stop in the middle of the road?
Because he wanted to be a banana split.

What did the cannibal have for breakfast?
Baked Beings.

What's a cannibal's favourite game?
Swallow the leader.

Did you hear about the restaurant on the moon?
Great food but no atmosphere.

What did the cannibal say when he found the hunter asleep?
'Ah, breakfast in bed.'

Why are cooks so mean?
Because they beat the eggs and whip the cream.

What did one plate say to the other plate?
'Lunch is on me.'

Have you heard the joke about the butter?
No, better not tell you, you might spread it.

'Johnny, this salad tastes awful, did you wash the lettuce like I asked you?'
'Yes Mum, and I used soap too.'

What cup can't you drink from?
A hiccup.

If a radish and a cabbage ran a race who would win?
The cabbage because it's a-head.

Why do bakers bake for a living?
Because they need the dough.

Why didn't the hot dog star in the movies?
Because the rolls weren't good enough.

How do monkeys cook their toast?
Under a gorilla.

What do you do if you find yourself stuck in a lolly shop with a bomb?
Grab a Life Saver.

Why is a cookbook exciting?
It has many stirring events.

Why did the girl throw the butter out the window?
Because she wanted to see the butterfly.

How do you make gold soup?
Add fourteen karats.

Have you heard the joke about the biscuit?
Better not tell you, it's too crumby.

What can a cook make with the letter 'Y'?
A cooky.

Did you hear about the big fight at the lolly shop last night?
Two suckers got licked.

What did Johnny's mother say when she saw him eat twenty pancakes for breakfast?
'Oh, how waffle!'

What do you get if you feed a baby too much cantaloupe?
A melon-colic baby.

Where do lollies come from?
Sweetzerland.

What is the egg capital of the world?
New Yolk City.

Why did the watermelon have a formal wedding?
Cant-elope.

Why is milk the fastest thing on earth?
Because it's pasteurised before you know it.

Heffalumps

'What do you call a group of elephants?'
'A herd of elephants.'
'Of course I've heard of elephants!'

What do you do if an elephant sits in front of you at the movies?
Miss most of the movie.

How do you make an elephant fly?
Push him off the top of a highrise building.

Where can you buy elephants?
At Jumbo sales.

What do you call an elephant that never washes?
A smellyphant.

What did the grape say when the elephant trod on it?
Nothing, it just let out a little wine.

What do you get if you cross an elephant with a biscuit?
Crumbs.

What do you give a sick elephant?
A very big paper bag.

Why aren't there many elephants at university?
Because so few finish high school.

What's the difference between an Indian and an African elephant?
Six thousand kilometres.

Why do elephants live in the jungle?
Because they don't fit in houses.

What do elephants play in the car?
Squash.

What do you get if an elephant sits on your best friend?
A flat mate.

What do you call an elephant in a telephone booth?
Stuck.

What happened to the elephant who drank too much beer?
He got trunk.

Why did the elephant go backwards into the telephone box?
He wanted to reverse the charges.

Why did the elephant tie a knot in his trunk?
So he wouldn't forget his hankie.

What is big, red and has a trunk?
A sunburnt elephant.

What do you get if you cross an elephant with a loaf of bread?
A sandwich you'll never forget.

What's the same size and shape as an elephant but weighs nothing?
An elephant's shadow.

What's the difference between an elephant and a grape?
A grape is purple.

When do elephants have sixteen feet?
When there are four of them.

Why did the runaway elephant wear green striped pyjamas?
So he wouldn't be spotted.

What do you call a hitchhiking elephant?
A two-tonne pick up truck.

Why are elephant rides cheaper than pony rides?
Because elephants work for peanuts.

How do you get elephants upstairs?
In an ele-vator.

What has four legs, eight feet and three tails?
An elephant with spare parts.

Why are elephants wrinkled all over?
Because they're too big to put on the ironing board.

How do you get an elephant out of a small car?
The same way you got it in.

How do you get five elephants into a small car?
Two in the front, one in the back and one in the glove compartment.

How do you fit five rhinoceroses in a car?
Chuck the elephants out.

What is grey, has large wings, a long nose and gives money to elephants?
The Tusk Fairy.

What is beautiful, grey and wears glass slippers?
A Cinderelephant.

Why didn't the elephant cross the road?
Because he saw the zebra crossing.

How do elephants talk to one another?
On the elephone.

What kind of elephant flies a jet?
A jumbo.

What do you get when you cross an elephant with a kangaroo?
Great big holes all over Australia.

How do you know if there is an elephant under the bed?
Your nose is touching the ceiling.

Why do elephants paint the soles of their feet yellow?
So they can hide upside down in bowls of custard.

'Do you ever find elephants in your custard?'
'No.'
'So it must work.'

Why weren't the elephants allowed on the beach?
Because they couldn't keep their trunks up.

What time is it when an elephant sits on your fence?
Time to get a new fence.

Why have elephants got trunks?
Because they can't afford suitcases.

How can you find an elephant in your bed?
Because it'll have a big 'E' on it's pyjamas.

Why did the elephant paint her nails red?
So she could hide in the strawberry patch.

What's the difference between an elephant and a flea?
An elephant can have fleas, but a flea can't have elephants.

Why did the elephant wear blue pyjamas to bed?
Because the yellow ones were dirty.

Knock Knock

Knock knock.
Who's there?
Who.
Who, who?
What are you an owl?

Knock knock.
Who's there?
Cows go.
Cows go who?
Cows don't go who, they go moo.

Knock knock.
Who's there?
Far out.
Far out who?
Far out man.

Knock knock.
Who's there?
Sawyer.
Sawyer who?
Sawyer lights on, so I thought I'd drop by.

Knock knock.
Who's there?
Freeze.
Freeze who?
Freeze a jolly good fellow.

Knock knock.
Who's there?
The Sultan.
The Sultan who?
The sultan pepper.

Knock knock.
Who's there?
Gotta.
Gotta who?
Gotta go to the toilet.

Knock knock.
Who's there?
Robin.
Robin who?
Robin you, so hand over your money.

Knock knock.
Who's there?
Roach.
Roach who?
Roach you a letter, did you get it?

Knock knock.
Who's there?
Olive.
Olive who?
Olive here. Who are you?

Knock knock.
Who's there?
Snow.
Snow who?
Snow good asking me.

Knock knock.
Who's there?
Major.
Major who?
Major answer a knock knock joke.

Knock knock.
Who's there?
Dwayne.
Dwayne who?
Dwayne the bathtub, I'm drowning!

Knock knock.
Who's there?
Isabel.
Isabel who?
Isabel necessary on a bicycle?

Knock knock.
Whose there?
Yah.
Yah who?
Ride on cowboy!

Knock knock.
Who's there?
Tank.
Tank who?
My pleasure.

Knock knock.
Who's there?
Turnip.
Turnip who?
Turnip for school tomorrow or you're expelled.

Knock knock.
Who's there?
Oscar.
Oscar who?
Oscar a silly question, get a silly answer.

Knock knock.
Who's there?
Ivor.
Ivor who?
Ivor you let me in or I'll climb through the window.

Knock knock.
Who's there?
Mandy.
Mandy who?
Mandy boats are sinking.

Knock knock.
Who's there?
Scott.
Scott who?
Scott nothing to do with you.

Knock knock.
Who's there?
Wood.
Wood who?
Wood you believe I've forgotten.

Knock knock.
Who's there?
Upton.
Upton who?
Upton no good, as usual.

Knock knock.
Who's there?
Granny.
Granny who?
Knock knock.
Who's there?
Granny.
Granny who?
Knock knock.
Who's there?
Granny.
Granny who?
Knock knock.
Who's there?
Aunt.
Aunt who?
Aunt you glad Granny's gone!

Knock knock.
Who's there?
Nanna.
Nanna who?
Nanna your business.

Knock knock.
Who's there?
Lion.
Lion who?
Lying won't get you anywhere.

Knock knock.
Who's there?
Las.
Las who?
That's what a cowboy uses.

Knock knock.
Who's there?
Bear.
Bear who?
Bear bum.

Knock knock.
Who's there?
Herman.
Herman who?
Herman eggs.

Knock knock.
Who's there?
Let her in.
Let her in who?
Better let her in or she'll knock your house down.

Knock knock.
Who's there,
Woo.
Woo who?
Woo do you think?

Knock knock.
Who's there?
Fang.
Fang who?
Fang you very much.

Knock knock.
Who's there?
Lettuce.
Lettuce who?
Lettuce in. It's cold out here.

Knock knock.
Who's there?
The boy who can't reach the door bell.

Knock knock.
Who's there?
Betty.
Betty who?
Betty late than never.

Knock knock.
Who's there?
Egg.
Egg who?
Eggslent.

Knock knock.
Who's there?
Nick.
Nick who?
Nick off.

Knock knock.
Who's there?
Luke?
Luke who?
Luke through the keyhole and you'll see.

Knock knock.
Who's there?
Will.
Will who?
Will you sit down and keep quiet please.

Knock knock.
Who's there,
Funny.
Funny who?
Funny the way you keep saying, 'Who's there?' every time I knock.

Knock knock.
Who's there?
Boo.
Boo who?
What are you crying for?

Knock knock.
Who's there?
Amos.
Amos who?
A-mos-quito.

Knock knock.
Who's there?
Mary.
Mary who?
Mary Christmas.

Knock knock.
Who's there?
Evan.
Evan who?
Evan's above.

Knock knock,
Who's there?
Adelaide.
Adelaide who?
Adelaide an egg.

Knock knock.
Who's there?
Canoe.
Canoe who?
Canoe please get off my foot.

Knock knock.
Who's there?
Barbie.
Barbie who?
Barbie Q.

Knock knock.
Who's there?
Caribbean.
Caribbean who?
You don't Caribbean that I'm standing out here in a storm.

Knock knock.
Who's there?
Carrie.
Carrie who?
Carrie me inside, I'm exhausted.

Knock knock.
Who's there?
Celia.
Celia who?
Celia later alligator.

Knock knock.
Who's there?
Dutch.
Dutch who?
Dutch me and I'll scream.

Knock knock.
Who's there?
Eiffel.
Eiffel who?
Eiffel down and hurt my foot.

Knock knock.
Who's there?
Harley.
Harley who?
Harley ever see you anymore.

Knock knock.
Who's there?
Hertz.
Hertz who?
Hertz me more than it hurts you.

Knock knock.
Who's there?
Justin.
Justin who?
Justin time for dinner.

Knock knock.
Who's there?
Kenya.
Kenya who?
Kenya keep it quiet down there?

Knock knock.
Who's there?
Nobel.
Nobel who?
Nobel, so I knocked.

Knock knock.
Who's there?
Rover.
Rover who?
It's all rover for you.

Knock knock.
Who's there?
Liz.
Liz who?
Lizen only once because I'm not going to repeat myself.

Knock knock.
Who's there?
Sancho.
Sancho who?
Sancho a letter, but you never answered.

Knock knock,
Who's there?
Satin.
Satin who?
Who satin my chair?

Knock knock.
Who's there?
Minnie.
Minnie who?
Minnie people want to know.

Knock knock.
Who's there?
Sue.
Sue who?
Sue-prise, it's me.

Knock knock.
Who's there?
Troy.
Troy who?
Troy if I may, I can't reach the bell.

Knock knock.
Who's there?
Dismay.
Dismay who?
Dismay be the last knock knock joke you ever hear!

Medical Matters

'The doctor told me to take these pills for the rest of my life.'
'So what's the problem?'
'He only gave me eight pills.'

What happened when the plastic surgeon sat too close to the fire?
He melted.

'The doctor has given me two weeks to live.'
'What did you say?'
'I said I'd take the first two weeks in January.'

'Doctor, doctor, I'm having trouble breathing.'
'Don't worry, I'll put a stop to that.'

'Doctor, doctor, my son swallowed a bullet.'
'Don't point him at anyone.'

'Doctor, doctor, my husband thinks he's a clock.'
'Are you sure you haven't been winding him up?'

'Doctor, doctor, my hair keeps falling out, can you give me something to keep it in?'
'Sure, what about this clean jar?'

'Doctor, doctor, come quickly! My boy has just swallowed a pen!'
'How are you managing?'
'I'm using a pencil.'

'Doctor, doctor, I've got beans growing out of my ears.'
'How did that happen?'
'I have no idea, I planted leeks.'

'Doctor, doctor, everyone hates me.'
'Don't be stupid, everyone hasn't met you yet.'

'Doctor, doctor, I've got jelly in one ear and custard in the other.'
'Don't worry, you're just a trifle deaf.'

'Doctor, doctor, Johnny's become a kleptomaniac!'
'Has he taken anything for it?'

'Doctor, doctor, I think I'm a billiard ball!'
'Go to the back of the queue.'

'Doctor, doctor, I'm suffering from hallucinations.'
'I'm sure you're only imagining it!'

'Doctor, doctor, can you give me anything for wind?'
'Sure, here's a kite.'

'Doctor, doctor, how can I stop smoking?'
'Stop setting fire to yourself.'

'Doctor, doctor, I keep thinking I'm a fruitcake!'
'What's got into you?'
'Flour, raisins, sultanas and cherries!'

'Doctor, doctor, I think I'm a goat!'
'How long have you thought this?'
'Since I was a kid.'

'Doctor, doctor, I feel like a bell.'
'Well take these, and if they don't work give me a ring.'

'Doctor, doctor, I can't sleep at night.'
'Well lie on the edge of the bed and you'll soon drop off.'

'Doctor, doctor, I've swallowed my camera!'
'Lets hope nothing develops.'

'Doctor, doctor, everyone keeps ignoring me!'
'Next please.'

'Doctor, doctor, I keep seeing green monsters with orange spots.'
'Have you seen a psychiatrist?'
'No, just green monsters with orange spots.'

'Doctor, doctor, I think I'm turning into a dustbin!'
'Don't talk such rubbish.'

'Doctor, doctor, I feel like an apple.'
'Don't worry, I don't bite.'

'Doctor, doctor, I feel like a pack of cards.'
'Wait here, I'll deal with you in a minute.'

'Doctor, doctor, I feel like a curtain.'
'For heaven's sake pull yourself together.'

'Doctor, doctor, I feel like a dog!'
'Sit!'

'Doctor, doctor, I keep hearing ringing in my ears.'
'Well, where did you expect to hear it?'

'Doctor, doctor, there's an invisible man in the waiting room!'
'Well tell him I can't see him!'

'Doctor, doctor, you've got to help me, I think I'm a bridge!'
'What's come over you?'
'So far two cars, a truck and a motorbike.'

'Doctor, doctor, I keep thinking no one can hear me.'
'What seems to be the trouble?'

'Doctor, doctor, my hands won't stop shaking.'
'Do you drink a lot?'
'No. I spill most of it.'

'Doctor, doctor, I get this really bad stabbing pain in the eye whenever I drink a cup of coffee.'
'Try taking the spoon out.'

'Doctor, doctor, I think I'm getting smaller!'
'You'll just have to be a little patient.'

'Doctor, doctor, you've got to help me. I just swallowed my harmonica!'
'Lucky you weren't playing the piano.'

What did the first tonsil say to the second tonsil?
'Better get dressed up tonight, we're going out.'

Did you hear the one about the boy who loved his operation?
The doctor had him in stitches.

I wanted to be a doctor but I didn't have the patients.

'Doctor, tell me, can a child of twelve take out his appendix?'
'Certainly not Madam.'
'Did you hear that Johnny? Now put them back!'

'I think you need glasses.'
'But I already wear glasses.'
'In that case I need some too.'

'You need glasses Miss.'
'How can you tell? You haven't examined me yet.'
'Well, I knew as soon as you walked through that window.'

A doctor had to inform a patient he had only a few minutes to live.
'Doctor, can't you do something?'
'Well, I could boil you an egg.'

A young boy arrives at the doctor's crying his heart out.

'Doctor, doctor, no matter where I touch myself it hurts.'

'Show me where you mean,' said the doctor.

So the boy touched himself on the nose and cried because it hurt. He touched himself on his chest and cried because it hurt. He touched himself on his tummy and cried because it hurt. And then he touched himself in another twelve places and every time it really, really hurt.

'What's wrong with me doctor?' he asked. 'How come I hurt all over?'

'Because,' said the doctor, 'you've got a broken finger.'

'Are you hurt?'
'Yeah, better call me a doctor.'
'OK, you're a doctor.'

Multiculturalism

Why did the Irishman drown?
Because he was practising his river dance.

What do you need to blind an Asian?
A flash.

'What have you got in your pocket?' one Irishman asks another.
'I'll give you a clue. It begins with 'N'.'
'A napple,' said the first Irishman.
'No, I told you it begins with 'N'.'
'A norange!'
'No, I'm telling you for the last time, it begins with 'N'.'
'Would it be a nonion?'
'You got it at last.'

'What's that on your shoulder, Paddy?'
'A birthmark.'
'How long have you had it?'

What do you call an aborigine in a Ferrari?
A jaffa.

What do you get if you cross a Japanese girl with a fish?
Sushi.

What has two legs, two arms and looks just like an Indian?
A photo of an Indian.

An American, a New Zealander and an Australian are sentenced to death. The American is bought out first. The firing squad takes aim. Suddenly the American yells: 'Avalanche!' In the confusion he escapes.

The New Zealander is impressed and decides to try something similar. As the squad takes aim he yells: 'Flood!' And in the confusion, he too makes his escape.

The Australian has observed this closely. He decides to follow their example. So just as the firing squad takes aim, he yells: 'Fire!'

A Chinaman, an Englishman, an American and an Australian are boasting about which country is the best. The Chinaman says: 'We've got the best country because we've got the great wall of China.'

The others say: 'What's so great about that?'

The Englishman says: 'We've got the best country because we've got the Botanical Gardens.'

The others say: 'What's so great about that?'

The American says: 'We've got the best country because we've got the stars and stripes.'

The others say: 'What's so great about that?'

Finally the Australian speaks: 'Look we've got the best country because we've got the kangaroo.'

'What's so great about that?' the others cry.

'Well, it can jump over the Great Wall of China, skip through the Botanical Gardens, and go to sleep on the flag.'

Why did the Irishman wear pearls around his neck?
So he'd know where to stop shaving.

Why was the Egyptian boy confused?
Because his Daddy was a Mummy.

How do you confuse an Irishman?
Give him a jaffa and tell him to eat the chocolate first.

A man walked up to a sheep farmer and said: 'If I can tell you exactly how many sheep you have down there, can I keep one?'

The farmer glanced at the vast array of sheep, and sniggered: 'Yep.'

The man looked over the sheep carefully and said: 'You have 2,471 sheep.'

The farmer was amazed: 'How did you do that?'

'I'd rather not say, can I have my sheep now?'

'Of course.'

The man picked up an animal and walked away.

'Wait!' called the farmer. 'If I can guess where you come from, will you give me back my animal?'

'Sure.'

The farmer waited a minute and then said: 'You're from New Zealand.'

'You're right, how'd you guess that?'

'Well, I'd rather not say, but can I have my dog back now?'

Why do Irish dogs have flat faces?
Because they chase parked cars.

How do you confuse a Pole?
Put him in a room and tell him to go to his room.

How do you confuse an Australian?
Put him in a round room and tell him to go to the corner.

What is a shark afraid of?
A Japanese tourist.

What took over Japan?
Cameras.

Why do Irish men wear two pairs of underpants?
To be sure, to be sure.

I'm an Australian born and bred,
Long in the leg and short in the head.

Naughtiness

The Queen was showing the Archbishop around her stables, when one of her prize thoroughbreds let off a huge, loud fart.

'Oh I am sorry,' said the Queen. 'How embarrassing.'

'It's perfectly all right Your Majesty, as a matter of fact, I thought it was the horse.'

Humpty Dumpty sat on the loo,
Humpty Dumpty did a big poo.

Mrs Jones took her poodle, Tits Wobble, for a walk and lost him. Finally she reported her dog missing to the police.

'Have you seen my Tits Wobble?' she asked the sergeant.

'No,' he said. 'But I'd like to.'

A man steps into an elevator, where a very dignified woman is standing in front of the buttons. He soon realises there's a bad smell in the lift so he turns to the woman and asks: 'Excuse me, but did you fart?'

'Of course I did, you don't think I smell like this all the time?'

A bear and a rabbit are doing a poo in the forest, when the bear turns to the rabbit and enquires: 'Does your poo ever stick to your fur?'

'No.'

So the bear wiped his bum with the rabbit.

'Doctor, I have a terrible problem breaking wind all the time. But fortunately they're not noisy, nor do they smell.'

The doctor made notes in his patient book,

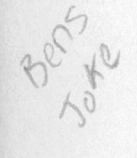

wrote out a prescription, and handed it to the lady.

'What's this doctor, nasal drops?'

'Yes, we'll fix your nose up first and then we'll try and do something about your hearing.'

An American tourist was driving across the Nullarbor Plain, when he saw a man sitting on the side of the road. He pulled up, opened his car door and offered the man a lift. The man declined, so the tourist shut the door and kept driving. For the next 500 kilometres he noticed that the man who said no to the lift was running beside the car. Finally he stopped again. 'Hey, are you sure you don't want a lift?' he asked.

'No.'

'How come you can run so fast?'

'You would too if you had your dick stuck in the door.'

What did Beethoven get when he ate baked beans?
Classical gas.

Why do farts smell?
For the benefit of the deaf.

'What do mothballs smell like?'
'How do I know? I can't find their bottom.'

Quickly, quickly, I feel sickly.
Hasten, hasten, get the basin.
Kerplop, get the mop.

What are hundreds and thousands?
Smarties' poo.

What do you call a smelly Father Christmas?
Farter Claus.

Why did the lobster blush?
Because the sea weed.

'Hold my hand. Now, how old are you?'
'I'm ten.'
'Where do you go to the toilet?'
'I use the public toilets.'
'How do you wipe your bottom?'
'I use my hand.'

Three children are smoking behind the toilet block.
'My dad can blow smoke through his nose,' says one boy.
'That's nothing,' says another boy. 'My dad can smoke through his ears!'

'So what,' says the third boy. 'My dad can smoke through his bum. I've even seen the nicotine stains on his undies.'

Oddities & Insults

signing yearbooks

A man was driving along a country road when he saw a sign up ahead saying DIP. 'Oh no,' the driver said, 'I forgot the chips.'

People like you don't grow on trees, they swing from them.

Three friends went skydiving, landed in the ocean and were eaten by a shark. Three hours later they all arrived in heaven. There they met an angel who said they could each make a wish. All they had to do was go down a slide and say what they wanted and it would come true. The first bloke went down and said 'gold' and that's what he got, the second said 'chocolate' and that's what he landed in, the third said 'weeee ...' and that's what he landed in.

I could say nice things about you, but I'd rather tell the truth.

If you ever need a friend, buy a dog.

There's a house with no doors, no windows, no chimney and there's a table in the room, how do you get out?
 Bang your arm against the wall until it gets sore. Saw the table in half – two halves make a whole. Climb out of the hole, scream until your voice gets hoarse, then hop on the horse and ride away.

Mary had a little lamb and all the doctors fainted.

What did one elevator say to the other elevator?
'I think I'm coming down with something.'

I never forget a face but in your case I'll make an exception.

I hear you're not allowed to visit the zoo because your face scares all the animals!

What did the hat say to the necktie? 'I'll go ahead, and you hang around.'

Went to pub
feeling nifty,
hit a pole
doing fifty,
poor old soul,
Doctor's fee,
cemetery.

I'd like to hear your opinion, but isn't there enough ignorance in the world already?

I'd like to make a formal complaint about you, but I hate standing in a queue.

'Here's a thousand dollars.'
 'What's this for?'
 'I steal from the rich and give to the poor.'
 'Wow! I'm rich.'
 'All right then, stick 'em up.'

'My watch needs a new band.'
'I didn't even know it could sing.'

Escaped prisoner: I'm free, I'm free!
Little girl: So what, I'm four.

You remind me of a goat that's always butting in.

I know I'm talking like an idiot. I have to otherwise you wouldn't understand me.

Have you heard the joke about the garbage truck?
Better not tell you. It's a load of rubbish.

Today all the toilets were stolen and so far the police have nothing to go on.

Most of us live and learn, you just live.

'You've burnt both your ears, how did that happen?'
   'Well, I was ironing when the phone rang.'
   'But how did you burn both of them?'
   'Well, as soon as I put the phone down it rang again.'

You're not really such a bad person, until people get to know you.

The next time you wash your neck, wring it.

There were three boys, Pig, Shut-up, and Manners. One day the three of them were digging for treasure when Pig and Shut-up found gold. Pig and Shut-up went to the Police Station. 'What are your names?' said the sergeant.

'Pig,' said Pig.

'I beg your pardon,' said the sergeant. 'Well, what's your friend's name?'

'Shut-up,' said Shut-up.

'Now listen you two, where are your manners?' said the policeman.

'He's running down the road with our gold!'

Beauty isn't everything, in your case it's nothing.

Your ideas are just like diamonds, very rare.

A full jumbo jet was flying over the Pacific ocean, when the pilot said: 'Ladies and Gentlemen, don't be alarmed, but our number one engine has just failed, we'll be all right but we'll be an hour late.'
A few minutes later: 'Ladies and Gentlemen our number two engine has just crashed, we'll be two hours late now.'
Five minutes later: 'I'm sorry to announce this, but engine number three has just failed, we'll still arrive, except it will be three hours late now.'
Two minutes later: 'Ladies and gentlemen, I'm sorry to announce this latest news, but engine number four has just collapsed.'

'Oh, no,' said the Irish passenger. 'I'm already late, now we're going to be up here all day!'

Look, you made a big mistake today, you got out of bed.

Watch how you sit down, you could give your brain concussion.

Your singing voice is OK if you don't like music.

You remind me of a one storey building. There's nothing upstairs.

If ignorance is bliss, you must be the happiest person alive.

I could break you in half, but who would want two of you?

It's not the ups and downs of life that bother me, it's the jerks like you.

What a shame you can't get anyone to love you the way you love yourself.

Don't complain about the tea, you'll be old and weak one day yourself.

You'd make a great football player, even your breath is offensive.

I hear your friends threw you a big dinner, what a pity they missed.

I can't believe your age, you must be older because no one gets so dumb so fast.

I've got a spare minute so tell me everything you know.

There was an old woman from Leeds,
Who swallowed a packet of seeds.
In less than an hour,
Her nose grew a flower,
And her hair was all covered in weeds.

You could improve this conversation by keeping your mouth shut.

I enjoy talking to you when my mind needs a rest.

There was a young man from Dungall,
Who went to a fancy dress ball.
He thought he would risk it,
And go as a biscuit,
But a dog ate him up in the hall.

You remind me of a jigsaw puzzle, so many of the pieces are missing.

You're obnoxious, mean, rude and ugly and they're your good points.

Little Miss Muffet,
Sat on her tuffet,
Eating her chicken and chips.
Her sister who's hateful,
Nicked half a plateful,
And strolled away licking her lips!

Got a match?
If I had a match for you I'd start a circus.

One more wrinkle and you could pass for a prune.

Your tongue is so long, when it hangs out people think it's your tie.

The only thing you ever give away is secrets.

Don't lose your head,
To gain a minute.
You need your head,
Your brains are in it.

No diet works for a fat head.

Better hide, here comes the garbage collector.

'Did you hear about the wooden car?'
'No.'
'It wooden go.'

I wish you were on TV so I could turn you off.

Wipe your nose, your brain is leaking.

'My cabin on the ship was OK, but that washing machine on the wall was hopeless.'
'That wasn't a washing machine it was a porthole.'
'No wonder I never got my clothes back.'

The only exercise you get is stretching the truth.

The more I think of you the less I think of you.

There were three tall men standing under the umbrella and none of them got wet. How could that be?
It wasn't raining.

You couldn't tell which way the lift was going even if you had two choices.

Look, where have you been all my life, and furthermore, when are you going back there?

'Dinosaur?'
'No.'
'Do you think he saurus?'

Every time I pass a garbage truck I think of you.

You must have been a surprise to your parents. Were they expecting a boy or a girl?

Why did the light turn red?
Wouldn't you turn red if you were caught changing in the middle of the street?

How many country and western singers does it take to change a light globe?
Three. One to change the globe and two to sing about the old one.

When I watch you eat, I know where they got the idea for *Jaws*.

The nearest you'll ever get to a brainstorm is a light drizzle.

People

Who made the first plane that couldn't fly?
The Wrong Brothers.

Why did Santa Claus grow a vegetable garden?
So he could go hoe, hoe, hoe.

'Hey farmer, what do you do with all the fruit around here?'
'Well, we eat what we can, and what we can't we can.'

If a steamroller ran over Batman and Robin, what would you have?
Flatman and Ribbon.

How do you confuse a gardener?
Take him to a room full of shovels and tell him to take his pick.

What do you call a flying policeman?
A heli-copper.

What does a farmer give his wife on St Valentine's day?
Hogs and kisses.

What is Beethoven doing in his grave?
Decomposing.

What game do spacemen play?
Astronauts and crosses.

Why does a cowboy ride a horse?
Because they're too heavy to carry.

Where did Captain Cook stand when he first landed in Australia?
On his feet.

What is Tarzan's favourite Christmas song?
'Jungle Bells'.

What would you call Superman if he lost all his powers?
Man.

What did the cowboy say to the pencil?
'Draw partner.'

Where do astronauts go for fun?
Lunar park.

What do astronauts make their pyjamas out of?
Saturn.

What's an astronaut's favourite food?
A Mars Bar.

What walks through the forest with sixteen legs?
Snow White and the Seven Dwarves.

Why are hairdressers never late for work?
Because they take short cuts.

What did Tarzan say when he saw elephants coming over the hill with sunglasses on?
Nothing, he didn't recognise them.

Where does Tarzan get his clothes from?
The jungle sale.

Tarzan flying through the air,
Tarzan lost his underwear,
Tarzan said, 'me no care,
Jane make me another pair.'

Boy flying through the air,
Boy lost his underwear,
Boy said, 'me no care,
Jane make me another pair.'

Jane flying though the air,
Jane lost her underwear,
Jane said, 'me no care,
Tarzan like me better bare.'

When is a farmer like a mystery writer?
When he's digging up a plot.

'Johnny,' said the dentist, 'you've got the biggest cavity I've ever seen. The biggest cavity I've ever seen.'
'Well, you don't have to repeat it.'
'I didn't Johnny, that was an echo.'

What's the difference between a well-dressed man and a dog?
The man wears a suit and the dog just pants.

What was Batman doing up tree?
Looking for Robin's nest.

How does Sherlock Holmes sneeze?
A-clue, a-clue.

What is green and plays the guitar?
Elvis Parsley.

What goes black, white, black, white
THUMP!
A nun rolling down the stairs.

What goes black, white, black, white,
ha ha ha.
The nun that pushed her.

What did the blonde call her pet zebra?
Spot.

How many jugglers does it take to change a light globe?
One, but it takes at least three light globes.

How many magicians does it take to change a light globe?
It depends on what you want to change it into.

What did Adam say on the day before Christmas?
'It's Christmas, Eve.'

What do you get if you cross Santa with a tiger?
Santa Claws.

Riddles

Why did the dog keep chewing the furniture?
Because it has a suite tooth.

What causes the death of a lot of people?
Coffin.

What word is always spelt incorrectly?
Incorrectly.

What do you call small rivers that flow into the Nile?
Juveniles.

What do you call a boomerang that won't come back?
A stick.

Where did they sign the Constitution?
At the bottom.

Can a shoe box?
No, but a tin can.

What's big, hairy and flies to New York faster than the speed of sound?
King Kongcorde.

Why does a steak taste better in space?
Because it's meteor.

What's black and white and red all over?
A newspaper.

Can February March?
No, but April can.

What is a specimen?
An Italian astronaut.

What are pilots' favourite biscuits?
Plain biscuits.

What is red and white?
Pink.

What colour is a shout?
Yell-Oh.

Why does a cat purr?
For a purr-pose.

Where do fleas go in winter?
Search me!

How do you make seven an even number?
Take the 'S' off.

What do you always see running along the streets in town?
Pavements.

What's an astronaut's favourite game?
Moonopoly.

What did one computer say to the programmer at lunchtime?
'Can I have a byte?'

What musical instrument is found in the bathroom?
A tuba toothpaste.

What's long, skinny and beats a drum?
Yankee Noodle.

What pop group gets your clothes cleaner?
The Bleach Boys.

What elf was a famous rock star?
Elf S. Presley.

What kind of music do you get when you drop a rock into a puddle?
Plunk rock.

What do you give a sick car?
A fuel injection.

What would happen if everyone had a pink car?
We'd have a pink car-nation.

What type of pants do scientists wear?
Genes.

What kind of phones do musicians use?
Saxophones.

What did the boulder wear to the party?
A F-rock.

What does your Nanna play records on?
The gran-ma phone.

What's the best way to cross a moat?
In a moater boat.

What happens when you kiss a clock?
Your lips tick.

What planet has the biggest bottom?
Sat on.

What did one petrol tanker say to the other petrol tanker?
'What do you take me for, a fuel?'

What lolly is always late?
Choc-o-late.

What do you get when you throw a piano down a mine shaft?
A flat miner.

How do angels answer the phone?
'Halo.'

Where do you study dancing?
At the disco-tech.

What sort of jockey do you see at the disco?
A disc jockey.

What is rude and only comes at Christmas?
Rude-off.

When do people with the flu get exercise?
When their noses run.

What do you get when you cross a computer programmer with an athlete?
A floppy diskus thrower.

What starts with 'P' ends in 'E' and has lots of letters in between?
A Post Office.

What do you call a fairy who never takes a bath?
Stinkerbell.

Which clown has the biggest shoes?
The one with the biggest shoes.

What kind of dress do you have that you never wear?
Your address.

What's faster, heat or cold?
Heat, you can catch a cold.

Why does the ocean roar?
You would too if you had crabs in your head.

What did the teddy bear say when he was offered dessert?
'No thank you I'm stuffed.'

What did the dirt say when it began to rain?
'If this keeps up, my name will be mud.'

How did the piano get out of jail?
With its keys.

What goes over and through eyes?
Your shoe laces.

What falls in the winter and never gets hurt?
Snow.

What did the paper clip say to the magnet?
'I find you attractive.'

What do you call a scared tyrannosaurus?
A nervous rex.

Why are flowers so lazy?
Because they always stay in bed.

Why do bagpipe players walk while they play?
To get away from the noise.

Why couldn't the bicycle stand up?
Because it was tyred.

Why did the bankrobber have a bath?
So he could make a clean getaway.

What kind of people live at the sea?
Buoys and gulls.

How do you get a baby astronaut to sleep?
You rock-et.

How do you start a teddy bear race?
Ready, teddy, go.

What has a bottom at the top?
A leg.

What kind of bow is impossible to tie?
A rainbow.

How do mountains hear?
With their mountain-ears.

What gets wetter as it dries?
A towel.

What's an Ig?
An eskimo's house without a toilet.

Why did the cleaning lady stop work?
Because she worked out that grime doesn't pay.

Why did the hand cross the road?
Because it wanted to go to the second hand shop.

What is always coming, but never arrives?
Tomorrow.

Why is playschool dangerous?
Because there's a bear in there.

What did the bell say when it fell into the water?
'I'm wringing wet.'

What are bugs on the moon called?
Luna-tics.

Why did the chewing gum cross the road?
Because it was stuck to the chicken's foot.

What sport do judges play?
Tennis, because it's played in court.

Who gets the sack every time he goes to work?
The postman.

Why do people laugh up their sleeves?
Because there are funny bones there.

What do fairys use to clean their teeth?
Fairy floss.

What do you put in a box to make it lighter?
A hole.

Why are tall people cleaner than short people?
Because they're in the shower longer.

What trees do hands grow on?
Palm trees.

What star can't shine at night?
The sun.

How do you get rid of unwanted varnish?
Take away the 'R' and it will vanish.

What sort of nails do you find in shoes?
Toenails.

Why did the sailor grab a bar of soap when his ship was sinking?
He was hoping he'd be washed ashore.

Where do astronauts leave their spaceships?
At parking meteors.

What kind of clothes did people wear during the Great Fire of London?
Blazers.

How do you make a bandstand?
Hide all the chairs.

What kind of ears does an engine have?
Engin-ears.

What did the piece of wood say to the electric drill?
You bore me.

Why is the sky so high?
So birds won't bump their heads.

What would you never find in a nudist camp?
A pickpocket.

What happened to the criminal contortionist?
He turned himself in.

Why did the pilot crash into the house?
Because the landing light was on.

What does the sea say to the sand?
Not much, it mostly waves.

Why did the man jump from the Empire State Building?
Because he wanted to make a hit on Broadway.

Why couldn't the sailors play cards?
Because the captain was standing on the deck.

What did the traffic light say to the car?
'Don't look now I'm changing.'

Why did the lady put a sock on her head?
Because she grew a foot.

What goes around the corner and stays in the corner?
A postage stamp.

What room can't you ever enter?
A mushroom.

Did you hear about the man who stayed up all night trying to find out where the sun went?
It finally dawned on him.

'I'd like a return ticket to the moon please.'
'Sorry, the moon's full tonight.'

What do you do when your smoke alarm goes off?
Run after it.

Why should you never marry a tennis player?
Because love means nothing to them.

What did the policeman say to his stomach?
'You're under my vest.'

Where did the inventor of the toupee get his idea from?
Off the top of his head.

Did you hear the story about the hospital?
No.
It's sick.

What letters in the alphabet are the best looking?
'U' and 'I'.

What can you hold without touching?
Your breath.

What has wheels and flies?
A garbage truck.

Why did the baby pen cry?
Because its mother was doing a long sentence.

Where does a general keep his armies?
Up his sleevies.

What sort of lights did Noah's Ark have?
Flood lights.

What did the cloud say to the sun?
'Don't move, I've got you covered.'

The more you take away the bigger it gets. What am I?
A hole.

Why is it hard to keep a secret on a cold day?
Because you can't stop your teeth chattering.

When is water like fat?
When it's dripping.

Have you heard the joke about the three wells?
Well, well, well.

Why did the milking stool only have three legs?
Because the cow had the udder.

What do you call two robbers?
A pair of nickers.

What do you do if your toe drops off in the middle of the road?
Call a toe truck.

When you lose something, why do you always find it in the last place you look?
Because you always stop looking when you find it.

Did you hear about the boy who ran away with the circus?
The policeman made him bring it back.

What do composers write in the bath?
Soap operas.

What burns longer, candles on a boy's birthday cake, or candles on a girl's?
Neither, they both burn shorter.

Did you hear about the man who didn't clean his glasses?
He gave people dirty looks.

What cars do hot dogs like driving?
Rolls.

What goes into the water pink and comes out blue?
A swimmer on a cold day.

What did one eye say to the other?
'Something's come between us that smells.'

What do you find up a clean nose?
Fingerprints.

Why is an old car like a baby?
It never goes anywhere without a rattle.

Why was Cinderella bad at football?
Because she had a pumpkin for a coach.

What did one ear say to the other?
'Between you and me we have brains.'

What goes up and wobbles?
A jelly-copter.

What is clear, but is seen by the naked eye and can be put in a barrel?
A hole.

What kind of music do mummies like?
Rap.

What goes ha ha ha ha THUMP!
A person laughing their head off.

What lies in a pram and wobbles?
A jelly baby.

Have you heard the joke about the bed?
It hasn't been made yet.

How do you make a hankie dance?
Put a little boogie in it.

What did Mrs Cook say when Captain Cook died?
'That's the way the cookie crumbled.'

What has a hole in the middle and no beginning or end?
A doughnut.

Do you need a hammer in maths?
No, you need multi-pliers.

What is the tallest building in any city?
The library because it has the most storeys.

What did one candle say to another?
'Are you going out tonight?'

What starts with an 'E' and ends with an 'E' but only has one letter in it?
An envelope.

What's the easiest way to get on TV?
Sit on it.

Why did the candle fall in love?
It met the perfect match.

How is a song like a locked door?
You need the right key for both.

What goes up when you count down?
A rocket.

If you invited all the alphabet to tea who would be late?
The letters 'UVWXYZ' because they all come after 'T'.

What do misers do when it's cold?
They sit around a candle.

What do misers do when it's really, really cold?
They light it.

What did the baby computer say when it got hurt.
I want my da-ta.

What is a computer's first sign of old age?
Loss of memory.

Did you hear the joke about the airplane?
Never mind, it just took off.

Did you hear the one about the express train?
Never mind, you just missed it.

Did you hear the one about the water bucket that had holes in it?
Never mind, I don't want it to leak out.

Did you hear the joke about the ocean?
Never mind, it's too deep for you.

What do you give someone who has everything?
A burglar alarm.

How do you keep from getting wet in the shower?
Don't turn the water on.

What lies at the bottom of the sea and whimpers?
A nervous wreck.

What has four legs and doesn't walk?
A table.

What did the shoes say to the socks?
'You're putting me on.'

Why did Cinderella get kicked out of the football team?
Because she ran away from the ball.

Why was number six sad?
Because seven eight nine.

What starts with 'T' ends with 'T' and is full of 'T'?
A teapot.

When is a car not a car?
When it's in a driveway.

If two is company, and three a crowd, what are four and five?
Nine.

What does the sun drink out of?
Sunglasses.

Where does Thursday come before Wednesday?
In the dictionary.

Why did the car stop in the middle of the road?
Because it was wheely, wheely tired.

What has many rings but no fingers?
A telephone.

What do you do when you wear your shoes out?
You wear them home again.

What did one hair say to the other?
'It takes two to tangle.'

How much does it cost a pirate to get his ears pierced?
A buck an ear.

Why did the heart get kicked out of the band?
It skipped a beat.

What has a hundred pairs of legs but can't walk?
Fifty pairs of pants.

Why are Saturday and Sunday so strong?
Because the rest are week days.

What did one phone say to the other?
'You're too young to be engaged.'

What did the jeans say to the bra?
'I'll meet you at the clothesline, because that's where I hang out.'

What loses its head every morning but gets it back at night?
A pillow.

Who do mermaids date?
They go out with the tides.

What is a ten letter word that starts with gas?
Automobile.

What is a waste of energy?
Telling hair raising stories to a bald man.

What is the best thing to take into the desert?
A thirst aid kit.

What did the apple say to the pear?
'Why don't you act like a banana and split.'

Why didn't the skeletons go to the movies?
Because they had no guts.

What is black and white and red all over?
A nun on fire.

What did the big chimney say to the small chimney?
'You're too young to smoke.'

Why do clocks seem so shy?
Because they always have their hands in front of their faces.

What did Cinderella say when her photos didn't come back?
'One day my prints will come.'

What's the difference between Cinderella and Tony Modra?
Cinderella gets to the ball first.

What can you serve but not eat?
A tennis ball.

What did one library book say to the other?
'Can I take you out?'

What did the cuffs say to the collar?
'Sleeve us alone.'

How do you make a fisherman's net?
Just sew a lot of holes together.

How do you say I love you in Italian?
'I love you in Italian.'

Why did the man pour veggies all over the world?
He wanted peas on earth.

What goes up when the rain comes down?
An umbrella.

When is a green book not a green book?
When it's read.

Which dinosaur knows the most words?
A thesaurus.

Do babies go on safari?
Not safari as I know.

When is a door not a door?
When it's ajar.

What do you call a dinosaur in high heels?
Myfeetaresaurus.

Scary Stories

Why did the sea monster eat five ships that were carrying potatoes?
No one can eat just one potato ship.

What do you say when you cross a two-headed monster?
'Hello, hello, goodbye, goodbye.'

What kind of lolly do ghosts like the best?
Booble gum.

What do ghosts wear when it snows?
Boooooots.

What happened when the monster ate the electricity company?
He was in shock for a week.

Where do ghosts put their mail?
In the ghost office.

What happens when a banana sees a ghost?
The banana splits.

What do you call two witches who live together?
Broom mates.

Why is the Jolly Green Giant a good gardener?
Because he had two green thumbs.

What's a skeleton afraid of?
A dog. Because it likes bones.

Why doesn't anyone kiss a vampire?
Because they have bat breath.

So, what is a skeleton?
Bones with the person scraped off.

What is Dracula's motto?
The morgue the merrier.

What do sea monsters eat for tea?
Fish and ships.

What do you call a skeleton who tells jokes?
Funny bones.

What's a skeleton's favourite instrument?
A saxa-bone.

What is a devil's picket line called?
A demon-stration.

What did Johnny ghost call his Mum and Dad?
His transparents.

Why do ghosts go to parties?
To have a wail of a time.

What do ghosts do every night at one a.m.?
Take a coffin break.

What's a vampire's favourite drink?
A Bloody Mary.

What is a ghost's favourite dessert?
Boo-berry pie with I-scream.

What did the ghost buy his wife for her birthday?
A see-through nightie.

What do you think the tiniest vampire in the world gets up to at night?
Your ankles.

Who is the most important member of the ghosts' football team?
The ghoulie.

How does a vampire clean his house?
With a victim cleaner.

What do you call a swarm of ghost bees?
Zombees.

What can a vegetarian cannibal eat?
Swedes.

If you want to hunt ghosts, what is the best way to keep fit?
Exorcise yourself.

Where do vampires keep their savings?
In a blood bank.

What job did the lady ghost have on the jumbo jet?
Lady ghostess.

Why did the ghost look in the mirror?
To make sure it really wasn't there.

What do ghosts eat for lunch?
Goulash.

When does a ghost become two ghosts?
When it's beside itself.

What do you call a play that's acted by ghosts?
A phantomine.

How do you make a witch itch?
Take away the 'W'.

What do cannibals eat at parties?
Buttered host.

What do you call a friendly, good looking wizard?
A failure.

Why do witches get plenty of bargains?
Because they love to haggle.

Why do ghosts hate rain?
It dampens their spirits.

Why did the skeleton run up the tree?
Because a dog was after his bones.

What's the first thing a ghost does when it gets into a car?
It fastens the sheet belt.

What do you call a skeleton that doesn't do any work?
Lazy Bones.

How long did the ghost plan to stay in Sydney?
Not long. He was just passing through.

Why are vampires stupid?
Because they're suckers.

How do ghosts like their eggs?
Terror-fried.

What do ghosts eat?
Dread and butter pudding.

How do ghosts learn songs?
With sheet music.

Which musical instrument does a skeleton play?
A trom-bone.

Why didn't the vampire want to play cricket?
Because he didn't want to damage his bats.

Why did the little girl eat a box of bullets?
She wanted to grow bangs.

What does a monster call his parents?
Deady and Mummy.

How does a vampire cross the ocean?
In a blood vessel.

A giant green monster from Blister,
Decided to eat up his sister.
And when he was through,
He cried: 'What did I do?'
Now he's sorry he did, 'cause he missed her.

Why do wizards drink tea?
Because sorcerers need cuppas.

What do you call a wizard from outer space?
A flying sorcerer.

What kind of jewels do monsters wear?
Tombstones.

'How many times Little Johnny monster must I tell you to play with your food before you eat it?'

What's a monster's favourite sport?
Squash.

What's a monster's favourite game at night?
Swallow my leader.

Why did Frankenstein have indigestion?
He bolted his food.

What do you call a city full of monsters?
A monstro-sity.

What medicine do ghosts take when they get the flu?
Coffin drops.

Why aren't vampires welcome in blood banks?
Because they only make withdrawals.

'Johnny Monster, I told you not to speak when you've got someone in your mouth.'

What do good monsters try to remember to say?
Fangs very much.

Did you hear about the bald-headed man who met a man-eating monster?
He had a hair raising experience.

Why did the vampire ask the ghost to join their hockey team?
Because they needed some team spirit.

What do you call ghost children?
Boys and ghouls.

What did the monster say when introduced?
'Pleased to eat you.'

Why did the monster fall in love with a piano?
Because it had such beautiful straight teeth.

A monster adrift on a raft,
Had never been on such a craft.
He fashioned a sail,
With his body and tail,
While the fishes around him just laughed.

What do you call a dumb skeleton?
A numbskull.

What do you call a skeleton who always tells lies?
A boney phoney.

Why did the two ghosts go to the scary movie?
Because they both loved each shudder.

What kind of dog does a ghost have?
A boo-dle.

What happened to the author who died?
He became a ghost writer.

What do ghosts eat for breakfast?
Shrouded wheat.

How does a ghost count?
One, *boo*, three, four, five, six, seven, *hate*, nine, *frighten*.

Why did the girl marry the ghost?
She didn't know what possessed her.

'I called the Vampire gang and told them the card game is on tonight at eight at the cemetery.'
'Why there?'
'Well, if someone doesn't turn up we'll be able to dig up another player.'

What weighs a thousand kilograms but is all bone?
A skele-tonne.

How do you make a skeleton laugh?
Tickle its funny bone.

What do you call a wicked old woman who lives on the beach?
A sandwich.

Why are skeletons usually so calm?
Because nothing gets under their bones.

What did the baby witch want for her birthday?
A haunted doll's house.

What did the ghost teacher say to the ghost student?
'You've lost your spirit.'

What motto do ghosts hate?
'Never say die.'

How many hamburgers do you give to a huge, mean monster?
As many as it wants.

What do women ghosts who have been in hospital love to do?
Talk about their apparitions.

Why are ghosts always drunk?
Because they're too fond of spirits.

What do you call a sorceress without a broomstick?
A witch hiker.

What did the ghost say to the other ghost?
'Do you believe in people?'

What's big and ugly with red spots all over it?
A monster with measles.

How do you tell a good monster from a bad one?
If you meet a good monster, you'll be able to talk about it later.

Where would you find a one-handed monster?
In a second hand store.

What do you do with a green monster?
Put it in the sun until it ripens.

Why are vampires like stars?
Because they only come out at night.

How do you greet a three-legged monster?
'Hello, hello, hello.'

What did the vampire catch after staying up all night?
A bat cold.

What do witches have for dinner?
Spooketti.

What do ghosts call their navy?
The ghost guard.

Why was the ghost arrested?
Because he was haunting without a licence.

How do you know when a skeleton is upset?
He gets rattled.

Why did the mother ghost take her child to the doctor?
Because it had boooping cough.

Why did the ghost want to go to Africa?
Because he wanted to be a big game haunter.

What do you flatten a ghost with?
A spirit level.

What do you get if you cross a ghost with a boy scout?
A boy that scares old ladies across the street.

Why don't monsters cross the road?
Because they don't want to be mistaken for a chicken.

What does a witch ask for when she books into a hotel?
'I want a room with broom service.'

Why does a witch ride a broom?
Because vacuum cleaners are too heavy.

'Mummy, I've got a stomach ache.'
'Must have been someone you ate.'

Did you hear about the stupid ghost?
He climbed over walls.

Where do ghosts go swimming?
In the Dead Sea.

What song do ghosts hate the most?
'Staying alive, staying alive, ha ha ha ha staying alive.'

How many vampires does it take to change a light globe?
None, they prefer the dark.

What's every monsters' favourite part of the newspaper?
The horror-scope.

How does a monster count to 13?
With one hand.

What happened when Frankenstein met a girl monster?
They fell in love at first fright.

What do you call a monster who eats his father's sister?
An aunt-eater.

Which street does a ghost live in?
A dead end street.

Who do vampires invite to parties?
Blood relations.

What do you call the winner of a monster beauty contest?
Ugly.

What's a ghost's favourite bird?
A scarecrow.

Why did Dracula go to the dentist?
To improve his bite.

What did the mother ghost say to the baby ghost?
'Don't spook until your spoken to.'

What games do you play at a ghost party?
Haunt and seek.

Why did they put a fence around the graveyard?
Because everyone was dying to get in.

'Who's that at the door darling?'
'It's a ghost!'
'Tell him I can't see him.'

What do you call the spot in the middle of a cemetery?
The dead centre.

What did the skeleton say to its friend?
'I've got a bone to pick with you.'

How do ghosts travel?
On fright trains.

There was once a ghost from Darjeeling,
Who got on the train bound for Ealing.
It said at the door,
'Please don't sit on the floor,'
So he floated up and sat on the ceiling.

What kind of spook can you hold on the end of your finger?
A bogey.

Why was Dracula lost on the freeway?
Because he was looking for the main artery.

What do ghosts put in their coffee?
Evaporated milk.

Did you hear about the ghost that ate all the Christmas decorations?
He got tinsellitis.

What is a ghost's favourite Christmas song?
'I'm dreaming of a fright Christmas.'

What happened to the wolf that fell into the washing machine?
It became a wash and werewolf.

'Hey brother ghost, how did you get that terrible bump on your head?'
'I was floating through the key hole when some moron put the key back in the lock.'

Why was the headless ghost sent to hospital?
Because he wasn't all there.

'Mummy, Mummy, tell me another story about the haunted house.'
'I can't little one, it was a one story building.'

What sort of society do vampires join?
A blood group.

There was once a young ghost from Gloucester,
Whose parents imagined they'd lost her.
From the fridge came a sound,
And at last she was found,
But the problem was how to defrost her.

Why don't ghosts make good magicians?
You can see right through their tricks.

When do ghosts haunt skyscrapers?
When they are in high spirits.

'Mummy, Mummy, am I a real ghost?'
'Of course you are, why do you ask?'
'Are you absolutely sure?'
'Of course! Why?'
'Because, I really hate the dark!'

Did you hear about the skeleton that was attacked by a dog?
It ran off with some bones and left him without a leg to stand on.

How do we know the letter 'S' is scary?
Because it makes cream, scream.

Why didn't the skeleton go to the dance?
He had no body to go with.

What does a ghost look like?
Like nothing you've ever seen before.

Why do demons and ghouls get on so well?
Because demons are a ghoul's best friend.

Why is Dracula a cheap person to take to dinner?
Because he eats necks to nothing.

Lady Jane Grey
Had nothing to say,
What could she have said
After losing her head?

What do witches put on their hair?
Scare spray.

How do vampires fall in love?
Love at first bite.

Where do ghosts go to church?
Westmonster Abbey.

What does a postman deliver to ghosts?
Fang mail.

Who is a vampire likely to fall in love with?
The girl necks door.

'I want a ghoul friend!'
'All right, all right, I'll see what I can dig up.'

'Do ghosts like the dead?'
'Of corpse they do!'

What is Dracula's favourite breed of dog?
Bloodhound.

Why do ghosts love living in high-rise buildings?
Because they have lots of scarecases.

What's the difference between a vampire with toothache and a rainstorm?
One roars with pain and the other pours with rain.

'I've just bought a haunted bike.'
'How do you know it's haunted?'
'Because it's got spooks on the wheels.'

What does a monster eat after he's been to the dentist?
The dentist.

How do ghosts begin a letter?
'Tomb it may concern.'

What do you find in a haunted cellar?
Whines and spirits.

What do vampires put in their fruit salad?
Neck-tarines and blood oranges.

What do little ghosts play with?
Deady bears.

How do skeletons communicate?
They use the telebones.

Where do cowgirl ghosts live?
In ghost towns.

Why wasn't the ghost very popular with the girls at parties?
He wasn't much to look at.

The ghoul stood on the bridge one night,
Its lips were all a quiver.
It gave a cough,
Its leg fell off,
And floated down the river.

What happened when the ghost went to the theatre?
All the actors got stage fright.

Five ghosts were sitting in the barn playing cards one windy night, when another ghost opened the door to come in and blew all the cards off the table.
 'For heaven's sake, why didn't you come through the keyhole like everyone else?'

What do you call twin ghosts who keep ringing doorbells?
Dead ringers.

What sort of eyes do ghosts have?
Terror-ize.

What trees do ghosts like?
Ceme-trees.

Who is Dracula's favourite composer?
Bat-hoven.

School Days

'Miss, can I go to the toilet please?'

'Yes Johnny, but I want you to say the alphabet first.'

'OK ... ABCDEFGHIJKLMNOQRSTUVWXYZ.'

'But where's the 'P'?'

'Running down my legs, Miss.'

'Welcome boys and girls to the start of a new year, now I want to ask you all some questions so I can get to know you better. Peter, what does your father do?'

'He's a fireman, Miss.'

'Paul, what does your father do?'

'He's a train driver, Miss.'

'And what does your father do, Johnny?'

'He's dead Miss.'

'Well, what did he do before he died?'

'He let out a groan, grabbed his chest and fell on the bathroom floor.'

What did one maths book say to another maths book?
'I've got more problems than you.'

Why did the teacher put her hands in the alphabet soup?
Because she was groping for words.

'OK class, who knows who defeated the Philistines?'
'The Swans?'

'Johnny, I hope I didn't see you looking at Mary's work then.'
'I hope you didn't too, Miss.'

'Johnny, put "gruesome" in a sentence.'
'I was short once then I gruesome.'

'Now Johnny, what's a comet?'
'A star with a tail Miss.'
'Name one then.'
'Mickey Mouse.'

What do you call a boy with a dictionary in his pocket?
Smarty pants.

'OK Johnny, give me a sentence with the word "indisposition" in it.'
'I always like playing centre forward because I like playing indisposition.'

What happened to the pot plant on the window-sill in the maths class?
It grew square roots.

Why did the science teacher put a knocker on her door?
She wanted to win the NoBell prize.

'Now that you've sat for your exams Johnny, how did you find the questions?'
'The questions were easy, but I found the answers hard.'

How do you know if your teacher loves you?
She puts kisses by your sums.

'Oh teacher, I would do anything to pass my exams.'
'Anything?'
'Yes, anything.'
'Well try studying.'

What's a good way of stopping pollution in schools?
Use unleaded pencils.

Why was the science teacher's head wet?
Because she had a brainstorm.

'Johnny, I told you to be at school by 9.15 a.m.!'
'Why, what happened?'

What's the difference between a teacher and a train?
A teacher says, 'Spit out that chewing gum!' And a train says, 'Chew chew.'

'Johnny, who was the first woman on earth?'
'Give me a clue Miss, please?'
'Well, think of an apple.'
'Granny Smith, Miss.'

Why didn't the astronaut go to space school classes?
Because it was launch time.

'Johnny, your homework is in your father's writing.'
'I know Miss, I borrowed his pen.'

'Now class, what is the difference between a stormy sea and this class?'
'We don't know, Miss.'
'A stormy sea only makes me sick sometimes!'

'Now class, who can tell me where you find elephants?'
'How can you lose an elephant?'

Why didn't anyone take the bus to school?
Because it wouldn't fit through the door.

'Now Katherine, can you spell kangaroo?'
'Cangaroo.'
'That's not the way the dictionary spells it.'
'You didn't ask me how the dictionary spells it.'

'Now, who can name five animals that live in the jungle?'
'One lion and ... um, um ... four elephants.'

'Now class, if I had fifteen chips in one hand and seventeen chips in the other, what do I have?'
'Greasy hands, Miss.'

Why did the boy take a car to school?
Because he wanted to drive his teacher up the wall.

Why was the teacher cross-eyed?
Because she couldn't control her pupils.

Why did the thermometer go to college?
Because it wanted to get a degree.

What do you call a teacher and twenty children?
A bolt and twenty nuts.

'Johnny, you missed school yesterday didn't you?'
'No teacher, I didn't miss it at all!'

'Now what's the letter after "O" in the alphabet?'
' "K"?'

'Class, class! I wish you'd pay a little attention!'
'Well we are,' said Johnny, 'as little as possible.'

Why did the boy bring a ladder to school?
Because he wanted to go to high school.

What do music teachers give you?
Sound advice.

'Now Johnny, what can you tell me about the Boston Tea Party?'
'Nothing, I don't think I was invited.'

'We're going to study the English Kings and Queens today. Now, who can tell me who came after Mary?'
'One of her little lambs?'

'Dad, there's going to be a small P&T meeting at the school tomorrow.'
'How small, Johnny?'
'Just you, me, and the headmaster.'

'Now, if you asked your mother for a dollar and then you asked your father for a dollar, how much would you have?'
'One dollar.'
'Can't you add up?'
'Well, Miss, you don't know my Dad.'

'Now class, there will only be half a day of school this morning.'
'Hooray!'
'The other half will be this afternoon.'

'Polly, did your mother help you with your homework last night?'
'No. She did it for me.'

What's the maths teacher's favourite instrument?
A triangle.

Why is a car like a classroom?
Because there's a crank in the front and nuts at the back.

'Daniel, if you had five dollars in one pocket and twenty dollars in the other, what would you have?'
'Somebody else's pants.'

'Teacher, can I get into trouble for something I didn't do?'
'No.'
'Good, because I didn't do my homework.'

'Why are you writing so slowly, Johnny?'
'Because it's a letter to my friend who can't read fast.'

'Johnny, it gives me great pleasure to give you 89 out of 100 for your science project.'
'Why not give me 100 out of 100 and really enjoy yourself?'

Sporting Events

Why do you need to take a cricket player with you when you go camping?
To help pitch the tent.

Why did the basketball player throw the ball in the water?
Because his coach told him to sink it.

Why shouldn't you tell jokes when you ice skate?
Because the ice might crack up.

What did one football player say to the other football player?
'I get a kick out of you.'

Why do soccer players have so much trouble eating?
They think they can't use their hands.

When is the best time to long jump?
In a leap year.

'Mum look, I've just found a lost football.'
'How do you know it's lost?'
'Well, the kids down the road are still looking for it.'

When is a baby like a basketball player?
When it dribbles.

What race is never run?
A swimming race.

'Hey Johnny, how come you don't have your football uniform on?'
'My doctor said I can't play football.'
'I could have told you that ages ago.'

Why did the policeman run across the baseball field?
Someone stole second base.

Why was Melbourne cricket ground so hot after the match?
Because all the fans had left.

'Why didn't you stop that ball, goalkeeper?'
'Well, I thought that's what the nets were for.'

Why were all the cricketers given cigarette lighters?
Because they lost all their matches.

Why are snooker players patient?
Because they don't mind standing at the end of a cue.

'Johnny, what are you doing home so early, I thought you had baseball practice?'
'I did, but I hit the ball over the fence and the coach told me to run home.'

What did the bowling ball say to the bowling pins?
'Don't stop me, I'm on a roll.'

Why is bowling called a quiet sport?
Because you can always hear a pin drop.

Why does a golfer always wear two pairs of trousers?
In case he gets a hole in one.

What is the ski instructor's favourite song?
'There's no business like snow business.'

Who can go as fast as a race horse?
The jockey.

Why does a football player always carry a spare pen?
In case he needs an extra point.

How does a hockey player kiss?
He puckers up.

What kind of dog is a fighter?
A boxer.

Why can't a car play football?
Because it's only got one boot.

'According to my watch, I can run 100 metres in ten seconds.'
'Yeah, my watch runs slow too.'

'How's the fishing around here?'
'It's OK.'
'Then how come you haven't caught any fish?'
'You asked me about fishing not catching.'

'I won't play tennis, it's just too noisy!'
'Noisy?'
'Yeah, everyone raises a racket.'

Why did all the bowling pins go down?
Because they were on strike.

Why did the jogger go to the vet's?
Because his calves hurt.

What Do You Call...?

What do you call a woman with one leg shorter than the other?
Eileen.

What do you call a girl with one foot on either side of the river?
Bridget.

What do you call a man with no arms and no legs floating out at sea?
Bob.

What do you call a person who's a talented painter?
Art.

What do you call a man with a spade on his head?
Doug.

What do you call a girl who gambles?
Betty.

What do you call a camel with no humps?
A horse.

What do you call a girl with a frog on her head?
Lily.

What do you call a person who's always around when you need them?
Andy.

Who was Russia's favourite gardener?
Ivan Hoe.

What do you call a man in a pile of leaves?
Russell.

Which rock singer has a vegie garden on her head?
Tina Turnip.

What do you call a woman in the distance?
Dot.

What do you call a lawyer?
Sue.

What do you call a man with a number plate on his head?
Reg.

What do you call a boy with a rabbit cage on his head?
Warren.

What do you call a man with a car on his head?
Jack.

What do you call a person who can sing and drink lemonade at the same time?
A pop singer.

Word Play

The Hungry Dog by Norah Bone

Cliff Tragedy by Eileen Dover

The Man Vanishes by Peter Out

The Ghost in the Attic by Howey Wailes

Walking to School by Mr Bus

Broken Window by Eva Brick

Ghosts by Sue Pernatural

The Omen by B. Warned

Poltergeists by Eve L. Spirit

Camel Rides by Mr Bumsore

A Hole in the Bucket by Lee King

Holidays in Britain by A. Pauline Weather

Infectious Diseases by Willie Catchit

Ghosts by I. C. Spooks

How to Grow Taller by Stan Up

How to Grow Shorter by Neil Down

Bell Ringing by Paula Rope

Tea for Two by Roland Butta

Driving through Germany by Otto Mobile

All About Explosives by Dinah Mite

Help for a Jail Breaker by Freida Prisner

Sahara Journey by I. Rhoda Camel

Rocket to the Sun by R. U. Nuts

Gone Chopin, Bach in a moment.
Out to Lunch, Offenbach sooner.

One One was a racehorse
Two Two was one too
One One won one race
Two Two won one too.

Four still standers
Four dilly danders
Two cookers
Two lookers
And one swish
That's a cow.

Good King Wenceslas looked out
From his kitchen winder
Something hit him on the snout
'Twas a red hot cinder.
Bright shone his nose that night
Though the pain was cru-el
When a poor man came in sight
Riding on a mu-el.

There are four people named Everybody, Somebody, Anybody and Nobody.

There was an important job to be done and Everybody was asked to do it.

Everybody was sure Somebody would do it.

Anybody could have done it, but Nobody did it.

Somebody got angry about that, because it was Everybody's job.

Everybody thought Anybody could do it but Nobody realised that Everybody wouldn't do it.

It ended up that Everybody blamed Somebody for what Anybody could have done.

I'd like to have your picture
It would look very nice.
I'd put it in the cellar
And frighten all the mice.

Little Miss Muffet
Sat on her tuffet
Eating her Irish stew.
Along came a spider
And sat down beside her
So she ate him up too.

If a blue house is made out of blue bricks,
and a yellow house made out of yellow
bricks, and a red house made out of red
bricks, what is a green house made out of?
Glass.

Mary had a little lamb
Her father shot it dead.
Now it goes to school with her
Between two chunks of bread.

Poor old Nelly's dead
She died last night in bed.
They put her in a coffin
And she fell right out the bottom.

Dr Bell fell down the well
And broke his collar bone.
Doctors should attend the sick
And leave the well alone.

Unfortunately one day a man fell out of a plane.
Fortunately there was a haystack under him.
Unfortunately there was a pitch fork in the haystack.
Fortunately he missed the pitchfork.
Unfortunately he missed the haystack.

The Thunder God went for a ride
Upon his favourite filly.
'I'm Thor,' he cried.
The horse replied,
'You forgot your thaddle, thilly.'

index

Aborigines 208
Adam and Eve 250
addresses 261
airplanes 243, 254, 271, 283, 368
alphabet letters 38, 132, 137, 139, 151, 274, 281, 282, 285, 324, 341
Americans 208, 209, 219
angels 260
animals. *see* different types of animals
ants 52
apes 33, 138. *see also* gorillas; monkeys
appendix 201
apple crumble 130
apple pies 133
apple trees 146
apples 116, 124, 198, 298
apricots 116
artichokes 120
Asians 207
astronauts 129, 131, 244, 245, 255, 256, 264, 269, 338
athletes 260
Australians 208, 212, 213
authors 310
automobiles. *see* cars

babies 92, 151, 264, 278, 292
bagpipe players 263
baked beans 147
bakers 149
baldness 98, 194, 288, 307
bananas 124, 127, 128, 130, 296
bandstand 269
bankrobbers 264
baseball 349, 350
basketball 347, 348
Batman and Robin 243, 248
bats 47, 48, 78
beaches 114
beans 113, 120, 195
bears 14, 19, 27, 49, 57–58, 69, 80, 218, 266. *see also* koalas; polar bears; teddy bears
beauty contests 319
bedbugs 51
beds 279
bees 19, 20, 22, 38, 54, 61, 63–64, 75, 76, 299
Beethoven 220, 244, 330

Bell, Dr 368
bells 197, 266
bikes 264, 327
bilby 70
billiard balls 195. *see also* snooker
birds 41, 56, 58, 60, 63, 144, 279, 290
birthdays 105, 299, 310
biscuits 116, 124, 126, 139, 143, 151, 155, 156, 255
bison 44
blondes 249
BO 99
boaconstrictors (snake) 26
boobies 110. *see also* tits
boogies 280
book title jokes 361–363
books 290, 334
boomerangs 253
Boston Tea Party 342
bottoms 221, 259, 264
boulders 258
bowling 350, 352
boxers 351
boxing 254
boy scouts 316
boys 358
brains 93, 102, 278
brainwashing 90
bras 288
bread 126, 140
breakfast 123, 129, 310
breath 274
breathing 193
bridges 199
brothers 94
budgies 44
buffalo 33, 44
bugs 266
bulls 15
bumble bees. *see* bees
burglar alarms 283
buses 339
butter 148, 150
butterflies 61

cabbages 123, 139, 149
camels 13–14, 25, 68, 356
candles 277, 281, 282
cannibals 147, 148, 300, 301, 316
cantaloupe 151, 152
car crashes 227
cards 198, 271
carrots 132
cars 70, 98, 109, 237, 257, 278, 285, 286, 302, 340, 343
catfish 83
cats 16, 18, 22, 27, 29, 34, 35, 42, 44, 46,

INDEX | **371**

(cats *cont.*)
55, 59, 67, 75, 78, 80, 95, 145, 255.
see also cheetahs; kittens; leopards;
lions; tigers
cattle 16
cellars 328
cemeteries 320. *see also* graveyards
centipedes 54, 62
cheese 115, 118, 136
cheetahs 41
chewing gum 267
chickens 23, 36, 41, 45, 46, 50, 56, 79,
115, 119, 125, 132, 140 *see also* chooks;
hens; roosters; turkeys
children 114, 308, 340
chimneys 289
Chinese 209
chips 340
chocolate 141, 144, 259
chooks 18
Christmas 103, 182, 221, 243, 245, 250,
260, 321
churches 326
Cinderella 278, 284, 290
circus 277
classrooms 343
cleaning ladies 265
clocks 194, 259, 290
clothes 269
see also cuffs; pants; socks; trousers
clotheslines 288
clouds 275
clowns 261
coffee 135
cold 261
collars 291
colours 255
comets 335
composers 277, 364
computer programmers 260
computers 256, 282
Constitution 254
Cook, Captain 245, 280
cookbooks 150
cooking 139
cooks 148
corn 115
cowboys 244, 245
cows 15, 16, 17, 18, 19, 24, 29, 31, 32, 35,
42, 43, 49, 63, 71, 74, 80, 81, 167, 364.
see also bison; buffalo; bulls; cattle;
steers
crabs 38, 133
cricket 78, 304, 347, 349
criminals 270. see also bankrobbers;
robbers; thieves
cucumbers 144

cuffs 291
curry 122
curtains 198

dads 333
Dalmatians (dog) 22
dancing 121, 260
dating 16, 127
deafness 195, 199, 220
death 227, 244, 253, 333, 368.
see also dying patients
demons 325
dentist visits 90, 248, 319, 327
deserts 289
dessert 298
devils 298
dicks 219
dictionaries 286, 335
dinner 314
dinosaurs 68, 75, 137, 239, 292
dirt 262
doctors 193–203, 368. *see also* plastic
surgeons
dogs 14, 16, 19, 20, 21, 22, 23, 24, 25, 26,
29, 30, 32, 45, 47, 49, 52, 53, 55, 56, 63,
65, 66, 68, 69, 77, 83, 91, 106, 198, 248,
253, 296, 302, 309, 324, 327, 351.
see also puppies
donations 97
donkeys 32, 73
donuts. *see* doughnuts
doors 292
doughnuts 140, 280
Dracula 297, 319, 321, 325, 327, 330.
see also vampires
dreams 89
drinking 125, 149
drinks 113, 125, 298, 305
ducks 17, 20, 24, 45, 65, 80, 117
dustbins 198
dying patients 193, 202

ears 195, 199, 229, 278, 287
eating 91, 93, 102, 114, 130, 147, 243,
304, 307
eating out 93, 99–100, 101, 114, 123,
133–137, 145
echidna 30
eggs 120, 125, 127, 137, 142, 143, 144,
148, 152, 177, 179, 303
Egyptians 210
electric drills 270
elephants 155–164, 339
elevators 226
Empire State Building 271
emus 56
engineers 270

English people 209
envelopes 281
escaping 226
Eskimos 123, 265
ethnic comparisons 183–188
Eve. see Adam and Eve
Everybody 366
exams 336
eyes 200, 277, 330

fairies 261, 267
farmers 247
farts 113, 218–219, 220, 221
Fatty and Skinny 109–110
fax machines 17
fingers 202–203
fires 90
fish 15, 34, 36, 37, 43, 65, 79, 84, 136.
    see also goldfish
fisherman's net 291
fishing 352
fleas 29, 60, 92, 164, 255
flies 60, 62
flowers 127, 263
flying 231–232, 243
food 88, 90, 113, 225, 303. see also different
    types of food
football 299, 334, 347, 348, 351.
    see also soccer
foxes 24, 37
Frankenstein 306, 318
frogs 25, 43, 44, 45, 57, 61, 62, 73, 77–78,
    103
frog's legs 134
fruit 243
fruitcakes 196

games 306, 309
garbage trucks 274
gardeners 243, 356
generals (army) 274
ghosts 130, 295, 296, 298, 300, 301, 302,
    303, 307, 309, 310, 314, 317, 319, 320,
    321, 322, 323, 324, 325, 326, 327, 328,
    329, 330
    bee 299
    child 308
    cowgirl 328
    headless 322
    mother 315, 319
    student 312
    stupid 317
    teacher 312
    women 312
    see also spooks
ghouls 325, 326, 329
giraffes 31, 39, 73, 76–77, 83

girlfriends 326
girls 355, 356
glasses, eye 202, 277, 285
glow worms 54
goats 34, 58, 66, 196
goldfish 49, 76, 140
golfers 350
gorillas 40, 47
grandparents 88, 91, 103, 105, 175, 258
grapefruits 118
grapes 138, 156, 159
grasshoppers 64
graveyards 320. see also cemeteries
Grey, Lady Jane 325

hair 98, 286, 325
hairdressers 246
hairstyles 88
hallucinations 196
hamburgers 145, 312
hands 266, 268
haunted places 323, 328
hearts 287
heat 261
hedgehogs 83
hens 20, 56
hiccups 149
highrise 327. see also skyscrapers
hockey 308, 351
hogs 53
holes 96, 97, 136, 268, 275, 279, 280,
    283, 291
Holmes, Sherlock 248
Holy water 146
home 92
homework 91, 338, 343, 344
horses 22, 30, 36, 64, 67, 68, 72, 73, 81,
    143, 351, 364. see also ponies
hospitals 273
hot dogs 149, 277
hotels 316
houses 367
hunger 121

ibis 56
ice skating 347
Indians 208
insects 99
Internet 36. see also World Wide Web
invisible man 199
Irish people 207, 210, 212, 213, 231–232
Italian language 291
Italians 255

Jane (Tarzan's girlfriend) 247
Japanese 208, 212
jars 121

INDEX | *373*

Jaws 144
jeans 288
jelly 279
jelly babies 279
jellyfish 20
jewels 305
jockeys 260, 351
joggers 352
Jolly Green Giant 296
judges 267

kangaroos 37, 55, 69, 70, 74, 162, 339
karate 28, 72
kids. *see* children
kittens 37
kleptomania 195
knives 129
Knock knock jokes 167–189
koalas 47, 48, 70, 72
kookaburras 46, 58

lambs 29, 141, 226, 342, 367
laughing 267, 279, 311
lawyers 357
leeks 146, 195
legs 264
lemons 145
leopards 15, 67
letters 274, 281, 285, 324, 341
lettuce 120, 131
libraries 280
library books 290
lies 90, 106, 123, 309
light globe jokes 57, 239, 249, 317
lions 13, 26, 46, 52, 82, 176
lips 98
lobsters 21, 221
lollies 151, 220, 259, 295
lolly shops 150, 151
long jump 348
losing things 276
love 273, 291, 326, 327, 336
lunch 126, 127, 128, 256, 301
lyrebirds 59

magicians 249
magnets 263
mail 326
marriage 310
Mars 109
Mary and her little lamb 141, 226, 342, 367
maths 280, 334, 335, 342, 343, 344
mayonnaise 119
meat 130. *see also* hamburgers; steak
medical jokes 193–203, 260
medicine 97, 307

melons 128
men 248, 355, 356, 357, 358
meringues 125
mermaids 288
mice 27, 35, 38, 55, 59, 76, 366
microscopes 101
milk 118, 138, 152, 321
milking stools 276
Milky Way 118
miners 259
misers 282
moats 258
money 94, 99
monkeys 30, 35, 55, 57, 67, 82
monsters 127, 131, 197, 295, 304, 305, 306, 307, 308, 312, 313, 314, 316, 317, 318, 319, 327
months 97, 254
moon 266, 272
mosquitoes 42, 61, 62, 181
mountains 265
mouse. *see* mice
Muffet, Miss 235, 367
mummies 279
mums 100
mushrooms 126, 131, 272
music 257, 280, 304
musical instruments 95, 96, 256, 258, 259, 297, 304
mustard 122

names 87, 103
navels 104
navy 314
Nelly 368
New Zealanders 208, 211
newspapers 98, 254, 317
Nile River 253
Noah's Ark 44, 275
nose picking 93, 278
noses 96, 106, 260
Notre Dame 126
nudist camps 270
numbers 256, 285, 310, 318
nuns 249, 289
nuts 124, 128

oceans 139, 262, 283, 305. *see also* seas
octopus 38, 79, 83
oil wells 100
onions 117, 125, 138
oranges 119, 132, 139, 140, 146
owls 40, 54
oysters 131

painters 355
pancakes 141, 143, 151

pants 89, 287. *see also* trousers
paper clips 263
parent and teachers (P & T) meetings 342
parents 304
parties 15, 20, 318
pavements 256
peanuts 120, 122
pears 289
pee 110, 333. *see also* wee
penguins 29
pens 274
people 95, 264, 267, 356. *see also* children; men; women
petrol tankers 258
phones 14, 18, 76, 287
pianos 15, 259, 262, 308
pickpockets 270
pies 132, 133, 142
pigs 25, 26, 28, 31, 55, 57, 66, 67, 70, 82, 145. *see also* hogs
pillows 288
pills 193
pilots 255
pineapples 117
pirates 287
piss. *see* pee; wee
pizza 115, 133
plane crashes 271
planets 259
plastic surgeons 193
playschool 266
polar bears 28, 41, 51
Poles 212
police 229, 230, 244, 273, 349
pollution 337
ponies 39
poo 110, 217, 218, 220, 221–222
pop groups 257
pop singers 357, 358
porcupine 46
post offices 261
postage stamps 272
postmen 267
potatoes 114, 116, 117, 120, 134, 140, 295
praying mantis 43
Presley, Elvis 248, 257
prisoners 228
prunes 127
puppies 19, 101

Queen, The 17, 217

rabbits 19, 32, 33, 35, 36, 45, 53, 72, 75, 82, 92, 218
radios 89
rain 29, 291, 302

rainbows 265
rats 65
restaurants 79, 147. *see also* eating out
rhinoceroses 40, 73
robbers 276
robbery 130
Robin. *see* Batman and Robin
rockets 281
roller blades 91
roosters 14, 41
rubbish 229
running 352

sailors 269, 271
salad bowls 119
salads 148
sandwiches 114, 121, 123, 129, 136, 311
Santa Claus 221, 243, 250
sausage rolls 124
sausages 134, 145
school day 343
school marks 344
schools 333–344
    missing 341
scientists 258
seahorses 67
seas 271, 284, 338
secrets 120, 275
shaking 200
sharks 39. *see also* Jaws
sheep 23, 27, 45, 64, 74, 80, 81.
    see also lambs
ships 237
shoe laces 262
shoes 66, 94, 284, 286
showering 284
sisters 102, 103
skeletons 289, 296, 297, 302, 304, 309, 311, 315, 320, 324, 328
ski instructors 350
skunks 14, 19, 21, 37, 38, 84
skyscrapers 324. *see also* highrise
sleeping 93, 109, 197
slugs 21, 136
smoke alarms 273
smoking 196
snails 24
snakes 16, 17, 28, 32, 41, 42, 47, 53, 779, 100. *see also* boaconstrictors
snooker 349. *see also* billiard balls
snow 263
Snow White and the Seven Dwarves 246
snowballs 39
soap 269
soccer 347, 349
socks 97, 99, 243, 284
songs 281

sorceress 313
soup 117, 119, 127, 133, 134, 135, 137, 150, 334
spaniels 14, 63
spelling 253
spice 130
spiders 51, 66
spinach 131
spooks 321
sport 306
squirrels 34, 36
St Valentine's day 128, 244
stars 268
steak 124, 132, 137, 254
stealing 228, 229
steers 15
stitches 201
strawberries 116, 144
streets 318
sun 268, 272, 275, 285
Superman 118, 245
survival 121
swallowing objects 193, 194, 197, 200
swimmers 278
swimming 95, 317, 348

tables 284
tadpoles 44
takeaway food 130, 141
talking 104
Tarzan 245, 247
Tasmanian devils 79
teachers 334, 336, 337, 340, 341, 343
teapots 285
teddy bears 262, 264
telephones 286, 287
television 16, 18, 281
tennis 267, 352
tennis balls 147, 290
tennis players 65, 273
thermometers 340
thieves 128, 141, 264, 276
thongs 103
Thunder God 369
tigers 31, 74, 128, 250
time 106. *see also* clocks; watches
tits 217
toads 31, 51
toenails 269
toes 276
toffee 122
toilets 221–222, 265
tomatoes 118, 122, 127
tomorrow 266
tonsils 201
tortoises 56

toupee 273
towels 265
Tower of Pisa 130
traffic lights 239, 271
trains 122, 283
trees 268, 330
trifle 117
trousers 96. *see also* pants
trucks 274. *see also* garbage trucks; petrol tankers
turkeys 20, 34
Turner, Tina 357
turtles 40, 49–50
tyrannosaurus 263

ugliness 105
umbrellas 291
undertakers 17

vampires 297, 298, 299, 300, 303, 304, 305, 307, 308, 310, 314, 317, 318, 319, 321, 323, 325, 326, 327, 328, 330
varnish 268
vegetables 114, 116, 117, 123, 129, 132, 140, 146, 291
vomit 48, 220

waiters 133–138
waking up 91
wasps 61
watches 228
water 275
water buckets 283
watermelons 127, 152
wealth 98
wee 221, 225. *see also* pee
wells 276
Wenceslas, King 365
werewolves 105
whales 39
wind 196
witches 296, 301, 302, 311, 313, 314, 316, 325
wizards 302, 305
wolves 322
wombats 70, 71, 74, 76
women 311, 338, 355, 357
wood 270
words 334, 335
World Wide Web 50
worms 16, 44, 113
wrecks 284
Wright Brothers 243
writing 94, 95, 344

zebras 82, 249